CHRISTIAN ROMAN EMPIRE SERIES

Vol. 13

THE LIFE OF SAINT AMBROSE

A TRANSLATION OF THE
VITA SANCTI AMBROSII
BY PAULINUS OF MILAN

translated with an introduction by
Sister Mary Simplicia Kaniecka

Evolution Publishing
Merchantville NJ
2019

Originally published by
Catholic University of America Press, 1928.
Copyright not renewed.

This edition:
© 2019 Evolution Publishing
Merchantville, New Jersey.

Printed in the United States of America

ISBN 978-1-935228-19-6

TABLE OF CONTENTS

Preface to the 2019 edition iii

Select Bibliography vii

Introduction xi

The Life of Saint Ambrose

Chapter I: The Author's Preface 1

Chapter II: Birth, Youth, and Early Public Career of Saint Ambrose 3

Chapter III: He is Elected Bishop of Milan, not without
the Will of God. He Tries to Evade but in Vain.
His Election is Confirmed by Miracles 8

Chapter IV: The Empress Justina Persecutes the Holy Bishop 14

Chapter V: He Finds the Bodies of the Holy Martyrs Gervase and
Protase, on which Occasion Devils are Driven from the Bodies
of the Possessed. The Blindness and Impudence of the Arians 16

Chapter VI: His Legation to Maximus the Usurper, and the Episcopal
Zeal against Him. He is a Terror to the Demons 21

Chapter VII: His Favor Prevails over Theodosius, Whom on
Account of the Massacre of the Citizens of Thessalonica,
He Deprives of Participation of the Sacraments. The Fame
of the Holy Bishop Reaches even to the Persians 24

Chapter VIII: He Firmly Resists Symmachus, the Prefect of the
City, Who Urges the Restitution of the Altar of Victory.
He Finds the Relics of the Holy Martyrs. Through His Favor
with God and His Authority, He Prevails over the Emperor
and the Queen of the Macromanni 30

The Life of Saint Ambrose

Chapter IX: The Virtues of the Holy Bishop. His Abstinence, His Zeal in the Divine Affairs, His Contempt for Riches, His Mercy toward Others. He is Resplendent with the Grace of His Blessings 42

Chapter X: He is Seized with Sickness and, Refreshed with the Holy Viaticum, Dies. The Funeral Rites are Celebrated by a Great Gathering of All. Demons are Witness to His Holiness. He Appears to Many after Death 48

Chapter XI: God Safeguards the Memory of the Holy Bishop against Detractors. An Exhortation on Imitating Him. The Author's Epilogue 56

Index 61

PREFACE TO THE 2019 EDITION

When Saint Augustine tells you to do something, you do it.

Paulinus, a deacon of the church of Milan in the early 5th century AD, received such a mandate from Saint Augustine, Bishop of Hippo Regius, following the death of a man who had been a spiritual father and mentor to both of them: Saint Ambrose, bishop of Milan. Augustine requested that Paulinus write a *vita* of Ambrose worthy of his lofty stature. For Paulinus, who by his own admission was not a gifted writer, the task must have seemed daunting. After all, Ambrose was one of the towering figures of his age, and attempting to capture his deeds and relate them worthily was no small task. As he admits in his own introduction, poor Paulinus did not even know the rudiments of how to craft such a work and Augustine had to provide him with examples to follow.

But for his many flaws as a biographer, Paulinus had two things in his favor that make his little *Vita* of Saint Ambrose an important work from both the historical and the spiritual perspectives. First, he was a member of the saint's inner circle. Paulinus spent years as Ambrose's secretary and was on intimate terms not only with the man himself, but with his family and friends, including his sister, Saint Marcellina. Second, Paulinus is by all accounts a good reporter and an honest observer. Many of the incidents he describes in this *Vita* he witnessed himself, or else heard from others who were close to the events. In many cases, the words and deeds recorded by Paulinus may be corroborated by the surviving correspondence of Saint Ambrose or other contemporary documents.

Further enhancing its value, Paulinus's *Vita* serves as one of the key primary sources for the most famous incidents of Ambrose's celebrated life. Among them are the few details we know of Ambrose's early years, including a picturesque account of a swarm of bees that settled harmlessly upon Ambrose as an infant. Paulinus is also the source for many of the details of Ambrose's unique conversion to Christianity and his elevation by acclamation to the bishopric of Milan even prior to his baptism. Also covered in varying degrees of detail are the numerous important political and ecclesiastical figures whose lives intersected with that of Ambrose including the Roman emperors Gratian, Magnus Maximus, Valentinian II, and Theodosius the Great, the Arian empress Justina, the usurpers Eugenius and Arbogast, the powerful magister militum Stilicho, saints like Augustine, Marcellina, Simplicianus, Bassianus, Venerius, and many, many lesser figures, some of whom are only known to posterity thanks to Paulinus.

This version of the *Vita Sancti Ambrosii* was rendered into English by Sr. Mary Kaniecka as part of her doctoral dissertation. Sr. Kaniecka's original edition suffered some criticism in academic circles, though as Andrew Lenox-Conyngham points out, it broke new ground and was not superseded for thirty years.[1] The *Irish Ecclesiastical Record* said that Sr. Kaniecka provided, "an excellent introduction, in which she makes a careful study of the style of Paulinus."[2] The translation is also perfectly suitable for students and interested general readers who comprise the core audience of the *Christian Roman Empire* series. For this new edition, Sr. Kaniecka's translation has been completely re-typeset with simplified punctuation, expanded bibliography, updated citations, and an index. It retains Sr.

Preface

Kaniecka's introduction and historical commentary, and includes numerous additional notes to help bring the text up-to-date. It has also been given a light edit to eliminate as much as possible the typographical errors that were criticized in the original edition. For the sake of brevity and focus, the present editor opted not to include Sr. Kaniecka's revised Latin text nor her detailed commentary specific to Paulinus's Latin grammar, syntax and vocabulary.

Since this translation appeared in 1928, other English versions of the work have been published, including one by John A. Lacy (1952) as part of a work entitled *Early Christian Biographies*, and another by Fr. Boniface Ramsey in his work entitled *Ambrose* (1997). Both of these books are worthy of consultation by the student wishing to place Paulinus's work in its literary context or to obtain a more complete view of the life of Saint Ambrose.

—Anthony P. Schiavo, Jr.
Merchantville, NJ
June 2019

NOTES

1. Lenox-Conyngham, Andrew. 1984. "Review of Paulin de Milan et la 'Vita Ambrosii' by Èmilien Lamirande" in *The Journal of Theological Studies, New Series,* Vol. 35, No. 1, pp. 240–242. Oxford University Press.
2. *The Irish Ecclesiastical Record.* 1928. Browne and Nolan: Dublin. Series 5, Vol. 32, p. 671

SELECT BIBLIOGRAPHY

Abbott, Frank Frost. 1901. *A History and Description of Roman Political Institutions.* Ginn & Co.: Boston, MA.

Ambrose. Roy. J. Deferrari (transl.) 2017. *Saint Ambrose of Milan: Theological and Dogmatic Works.* Ex Fontibus Co.: Indiana.

Ambrose. J. H. W. G. Liebeschuetz (transl.) 2005. *Ambrose of Milan: Political Letters and Speeches.* Liverpool University Press: Liverpool, UK.

Ambrose. Michael P. McHugh (transl.) 1972. *Saint Ambrose: Seven Exegetical Works.* Catholic University of America Press: Washington, DC.

Ambrose. H. Walford (ed.) 1881. *The Letters of Saint Ambrose, Bishop of Milan.* James Parker and Co.: London.

Athanasius. Robert T. Meyer (transl.) 1950. *The Life of Saint Anthony.* Newman Press: New York.

Augustine. H. Bettenson (transl.) 1972. *City of God.* Penguin Books: London.

Augustine. R. S. Pine-Coffin (transl.) 1961. *Confessions.* Penguin Books: London.

Augustine. Boniface Ramsey (transl.) 2008. *Responses to Miscellaneous Questions.* New City Press: New York.

Augustine. Philip Schaff and Henry Wace (eds.) 1887. *A Select Library of Nicene and Post-Nicene Fathers of the Christian Church, Second Series, Volume 5: Saint Augustin: Anti-Pelegian Writings.* Christian Literature Company: New York.

Baedeker, Karl. 1913. *Baedeker's Northern Italy.* Charles Scribner's Sons: New York.

Basil the Great. Agnes C. Way (transl.) 1955. *Letters, Volume 2.* Catholic University of America Press: Washington, DC.

Bingham, J. *Antiquities of the Christian Church, Volume I,* Reeves and Turner: London.

Boak, Arthur E. R. and James E. Dunlap. 1924. *Two Studies in Later Roman and Byzantine Administration.* Macmillan: New York.

Bouvy, E. "Paulin de Milan," *Revue Augustinienne,* vol. 1 (1902), p. 499.

Bury, J. B. 1911. *The Cambridge Medieval History, Volume 1: The Christian Roman Empire and the Foundation of the Teutonic Kingdoms.* Cambridge University Press, Cambridge, UK.

Cabrol, Fernand. 1907. *Dictionnaire D'archéologie Chrétienne et de Liturgie.* Letouzey et Ané: Paris.

Clausse, G. 1898. *Basiliques et Mosaiques Chrétiennes.* Paris.

Deferrari, R. 1952. *Early Christian Biographies.* Catholic University of America Press: Washington, DC.

Deferrari, R. 1922. "St. Augustine's Method of Composing and Delivering Sermons." *The American Journal of Philology,* 43(2), 97–123. JSTOR, www.jstor.org/stable/289454.

Dudden, F. Homes. 1935. *The Life and Times of Saint Ambrose.* Clarendon Press: Oxford, UK.

Farrar, Frederic William. 1889. *Lives of the Fathers: Sketches of Church History in Biography.* Adam & Charles Black: Edinburgh.

Greenidge, A. H. J. 1899. *The Student's Gibbon: A History of the Decline and Fall of the Roman Empire Abridged from the Original Work by Sir William Smith.* John Murray: London.

Hefele, Charles Joseph. H. Leclercq (transl.). 1907. *Histoire des Conciles.* Letouzey et Ané: Paris.

Herbermann, Charles G., et al. 1913. *The Catholic Encyclopedia: An International Work of Reference on the Constitution, Doctrine, Discipline, and History of the Catholic Church.* The Encyclopedia Press: New York. Electronic edition available at: http://www.newadvent.org/cathen/

Hitchcock, F. R. Montgomery. 1948. "Venerius, Bishop of Milan—II." *Hermathena,* No. 71, 19–35.

Hodgkin, Thomas. 1880. *Italy and Her Invaders, 376–476, Volume 1. Book 1: The Visigothic Invasion.* Clarendon Press: Oxford, UK.

Honoré, Léon. 1924. *Le Secret de la Confession. Étude Historico-Canonique.* Charles Beyaert: Bruges.

Jerome. Philip Schaff and Henry Wace (eds.) 1893. *A Select Library of Nicene and Post-Nicene Fathers of the Christian Church, Second Series, Volume 6: Saint Jerome, Letters and Select Works.* Christian Literature Company: New York.

John Chrysostom. Robert C. Hill (transl.). 1990. *Homilies on Genesis, 18–45.* Catholic University of America Press: Washington, DC.

John Chrysostom. Paul W. Harkins (transl.). 1984. *On the Incomprehensible Nature of God.* Catholic University of America Press: Washington, DC.

Labriolle, Pierre de. 1908. *Saint Ambroise.* Bloud: Paris.

Lapide, Cornelius. 1875. *Commentarii in Sacrum Scripturam.* Berche & Tralin: Paris.

Lenox-Conyngham, Andrew. 1982. "The Topography of the Basilica Conflict of ad 385/6 in Milan," in *Historia: Zeitschrift für Alte Geschicte,* Vol. 31, No. 3, pp. 353–363. *JSTOR,* www.jstor.org/stable/4435816.

Select Bibliography

Lesetre, H. 1883. *La Sainte Bible: Livre des Psaumes.* Paris.

Lowrie, Walter. 1901. *Monuments of the Early Church.* The MacMillan Company: London.

Mansi, Joannes Dominicus. 1759. *Sacrorum Conciliorum Nova et Amplissima Collectio.* Expensis Antoniizata: Florence, Italy.

McCauley, Leo P., John J. Sullivan, Martin R. P. McGuire and Roy J. Deferrari (transl.) 1968. *Funeral Orations by Saint Gregory Nazianzen and Saint Ambrose.* The Catholic University of America Press: Washington, DC.

McLynn, Neil B. 1994. *Ambrose of Milan: Church and Court in a Christian Capital.* University of California Press: Berkeley, CA.

Peck, Harry T. 1897. *Harper's Dictionary of Classical Literature and Antiquities.* Harper & Brothers: New York.

Priscus. John Given (transl.) 2014. *The Fragmentary History of Priscus: Attila, the Huns and the Roman Empire, AD 430-476.* Evolution Publishing: Merchantville, NJ.

Ramsey, Boniface. 1997. *Ambrose.* Routledge: London.

Rauschen, Gerhard. 1897. *Jahrbücher der Christlichen Kirche unter dem Kaiser Theodosius dem Grossen.* Herdersche Verlagshandlung: Vienna.

Scott, S. P. 1932. *The Civil Law, Including the Twelve Tables, The Institutes of Gaius, The Rules of Ulpian, The Opinions of Paulus, The Enactments of Justinian, and the Constitutions of Leo.* The Central Trust Company, Cincinnati, OH.

Smith, Henry. 1849. *Dictionary of Greek and Roman Biography and Mythology,* Little, Brown and Company: Boston, MA.

Smith, Henry and William Wace. 1887. *A Dictionary of Christian Biography, Literature, Sects and Doctrines.* Little, Brown and Company: Boston, MA.

Sozomen. Edward Walford (transl.) 2018. *The Ecclesiastical History of Sozomen: From AD 324 to AD 425.* Evolution Publishing: Merchantville, NJ.

Sulpicius Severus. Philip Burton (ed.) 2017. *Sulpicius Severus' Vita Martini.* Oxford University Press: Oxford, UK.

Sulpicius Severus. Philip Schaff and Henry Wace (eds.) 1894. *A Select Library of Nicene and Post-Nicene Fathers of the Christian Church, Second Series, Volume 11: Sulpitius Severus, Vincent of Lerins, John Cassian.* Christian Literature Company: New York.

INTRODUCTION

I. THE LIFE OF PAULINUS OF MILAN[1]

1. Early Life and Training

Of the life of Paulinus we know very little. Apart from his relations with Saint Ambrose and the Pelagian controversy, Paulinus is practically unknown. Bouvy[2] states, without indicating his source, that he became one of the group of religious at the *Presbyterium* of Milan whilst yet young and that this brought him into close relationship with Saint Ambrose, whose secretary he became in 395. After Saint Ambrose's death he is mentioned[3] as a firm controversialist opposing the Pelagian heresy in Africa. Where he came from and how he came to enter the *Presbyterium* of Saint Ambrose must remain matters of conjecture, but we may reasonably suppose with Schoenemann[4] that he was born at Milan or at least came to that city at a comparatively early age.

The date of Paulinus's birth cannot be arrived at even approximately, since there is no reference even to the time when he entered Saint Ambrose's school, and the scant details of his life that are recorded appear to be matters of inference rather than established facts. There is reason to believe, however, that he flourished between AD 375 and 422, since Saint Ambrose founded the *Presbyterium* about the year 375 and, as we have noted above, Paulinus entered it at an early age,[5] and because 422 is considered the latest probable date for the composition of the *Vita Sancti Ambrosii* and Paulinus is entirely lost to history after this date.

In speaking of the of the education of Paulinus we must treat briefly of the *Presbyterium* of Saint Ambrose, founded at Milan, in which Paulinus received his ecclesiastical training. This *Presbyterium* resembled a monastery in which Saint Ambrose gathered about himself certain men of the Church, living with them that community life for which our Lord had given the example and in which the holy bishop found great strength and personal joy. "It is a group of angels," writes he,[6] "where one is occupied only in praising and serving God." Among the members, those priests and deacons already matured, such as Castus and Polemius who remained deacons, and Venerius who later became bishop of Milan, and Saint Felix the bishop of Bologna,[7] helped Saint Ambrose in various ways. The rest, younger and less advanced in orders, were under the direction of a deacon. In this ecclesiastical school then, and under the care of the deacon Castus, Paulinus of Milan tells us[8] that he was prepared for the fulfillment of his divine vocation.

According to Saint Isidore, bishop of Seville,[9] Paulinus of Milan was raised to the dignity of the priesthood. It is possible that Paulinus could have attained this dignity in the latter part of his life, but that he was a religious of the Church of Milan with minor orders, we know from his own writings.[10] Marius Mercator[11] and Saint Augustine,[12] who knew Paulinus well, tell us that in time he received the rank of a deacon. Baronius conjectures[13] that Paulinus was honored with the diaconate later in life, being still at the death of Saint Ambrose the holder of minor orders. This would be consistent with Paulinus's own statements as well as those of Marius Mercator and Saint Augustine. In connection with the Pelagian controversy he is always referred to as Paulinus, deacon of Milan, and the fact that no more mention is made of his progress in the Church indicates that he never attained the higher honor of the priesthood.

2. Paulinus and Saint Ambrose

The very fact that Saint Augustine requested Paulinus to act as a historian of his master indicates much about the relationship that existed between Saint Ambrose and his secretary. That Paulinus formed part of the official retinue of the Bishop Ambrose is evident from the *Vita*[14] where our author, while recording the events of the year 395, makes mention of himself as being present and actually assisting at the finding of the bodies of Saints Nazarius and Celsus. On another occasion Paulinus relates[15] that he followed Ambrose to the palace "by virtue of our office," which shows that Paulinus really attended Ambrose in an official capacity. In 397 he was, in fact, Ambrose's secretary, for he tells us[16] that a few days before the bishop took to his bed he was dictating to him the 43rd Psalm.

Furthermore, the *Vita* contains evidence from which we may conclude that Paulinus was more to Saint Ambrose than a mere official, in fact that he was on intimate terms of friendship with the great bishop. Thus we hear of Paulinus consoling Saint Ambrose when he wept over the death of a bishop.[17] Again the reader is impressed by numerous personal touches. For example, Paulinus recognizes[18] in Saint Ambrose a man of great asceticism and prayer, a devoted and sympathetic father of the poor and unfortunate, a zealous and watchful shepherd, a daily example to all who surrounded him. Paulinus was ever ready to stand in defense of his loving master, and on a certain occasion in Carthage, about fifteen or twenty years after the death of Saint Ambrose, as we read in the *Vita*,[19] he energetically defended the outraged memory of the good bishop. In short, there runs through the *Vita* a warmth of feeling for Saint Ambrose which could only spring from a deep and intimate friendship between him and his biographer.

3. Paulinus After the Death of Saint Ambrose

Sometime after the death of Saint Ambrose, Paulinus went to Africa and made his home there, as is evident from the *Vita*.[20] In what city he took up his abode there is no mention, but we are certain that he spent some time in Carthage, since it was here that he met Cœlestius, the companion of Pelagius, and that he brought the heretical doctrines of the former to the attention of Aurelius, then bishop of Carthage. It was likewise in Carthage, while at a banquet in the home of Fortunatus, the brother of Bishop Aurelius,[21] that he defended Saint Ambrose against the detractions of Bishop Muranus. It was perhaps while he was in Africa that Saint Augustine asked him to write the biography of Saint Ambrose.

Just as the early life of Paulinus is practically unknown, the same may be said about his last days. We know that he took an active part in the Pelagian controversy, which is treated at length below. But once this heresy was crushed in Africa and the Pelagian controversy ended, the historians make no further mention of Paulinus.

II. LITERARY ACTIVITY OF PAULINUS

Of the writings of Paulinus only two of undisputed authorship have come down to us: *The Vita Sancti Ambrosii* and the *Libellus aduersus Cœlestium Zosimo Papæ oblatus*. A further work, the *Libellus de benedictionibus partriarcharum*, had been ascribed to Paulinus but his authorship of this work is now disproved. Before taking up the *Vita*, the chief object of our study, let us briefly consider the two *Libelli*.

INTRODUCTION

1. *Libellus Aduersus Cœlestium Zosimo Papæ oblatus*

Paulinus, as we have mentioned above, took part in opposing vehemently the Pelagian heresy, the originator of which was a certain Pelagius, of whom very little is known prior to the heresy. Perhaps this Pelagian heresy would not have taken such a deep root had it not been for Cœlestius, a friend of Pelagius, a man of restless and aggressive character. In AD 411 Pelagius and Cœlestius, after a stay in Rome, traveled to Sicily and Africa. Pelagius, after a brief sojourn in North Africa, went to Palestine, and Cœlestius tried to have himself made presbyter of Carthage. Here he began to spread the Pelagian doctrine freely through the city, filling all with dissension. Paulinus, seeing this, warned Aurelius, bishop of Carthage, that Cœlestius was teaching error and quoted from his writings seven distinct or inferential propositions, which he declared to be heretical. Saint Augustine[22] and Marius Mercator[23] relate the perverse doctrine of which Paulinus accused Cœlestius. Cœlestius, when ordered to renounce these doctrines by the bishops of a synod held at Carthage,[24] refused to do so and was excommunicated by the same synod.[25]

From Marius Mercator[26] we learned that as this heretic did not recognize the sentence passed against him by the bishops of Africa, he appealed to the Apostolic See. Pope Zosimus, the successor of Pope Innocent I, gave ear to the appeals of Cœlestius and summoned in AD 417 the deacon Paulinus, his accuser of five years before, to an interview.[27] Paulinus then, instead of appearing in person, sent Pope Zosimus a letter, justifying his attitude towards Cœlestius. This letter has come down to us under the title: *Libellus aduersus Cœlestium Zosimo Papæ oblatus.*[28]

This *Libellus* or letter is very brief. It is written, according to some historians,[29] on the 8th of November,

AD 416. Baronius,[30] however, places its date a year later. In this letter, the author sets forth his reasons for not appearing at Rome in person but also thanks Pope Zosimus, not only because he condemned Cœlestius but because he had asked that Cœlestius should renounce the false doctrines with which Paulinus had charged him. Paulinus, in this *Libellus*, does not give evidence of any great theological depth or learning, his chief argument being that of authority. Still his vigilance and firm stand against Cœlestius helped in some degree to crush Pelagianism in Africa.

2. *Libellus de Benedictionibus Partriarcharum*

Isidore of Seville states in his *De Viris Illustribus*[31] that Paulinus, a presbyter of Milan, wrote a book entitled *De Benedictionibus Partriarcharum* in which he sought to interpret the text of Genesis 49 in a threefold sense (*triplex intelligentia*). Isidore's authority was accepted by all subsequent writers before Tillemont. The latter states[32] that Isidore falsely attributed this work to Paulinus. Yet in 1751 Mingarelli published the *Libellus de Benedictionibus Partriarcharum* and, on the strength of Isidore's statement, ascribed it to Paulinus of Milan. However, this work is concerned only with an interpretation in a twofold sense: the "*sensus litterarius*" (*historia*) and the "*sensus allegoricus*" (spiritalis intelligentia).[33] Hence it does not correspond to the work described by Isidore and therefore has no connection with Paulinus of Milan. In all probability, the *Libellus* in question, on the basis of definite MS. evidence discovered several years ago by Wilmart,[34] should be assigned to Adrevald of Fleury-sur-Loire, who died in 878 or 879. As Bardenhewer says,[35] Isidore has again made a mistake. He seems to have had in mind the exegetical treatise *De Benedictionibus Partriarcharum* of Rufinus of Aquileia in which a threefold interpretation was given (*sensus historialis, mysticus, moralis.*)

III. THE TEXT

The text of this edition is based upon the so-called Benedictine edition of J. de Frische and N. le Nourry, *Sancti Ambrosii opera omnia*, 2 vols., fol., Paris, 1686–1690, with such charges as the readings of four MSS. would seem to justify. The MSS., three from the Bibliothèque Nationale, Paris, and one from Pembroke College, Cambridge, England, were collated from photostatic copies. A description of each of the four MSS. is as follows:[36]

A—Bibliotheca Patrium Latinorum Britannica, B 2.13 ch., sæc. XV (1462). Paulinus de uita S. Ambrosii. On the whole, it is carefully written and the text is complete.

B—Bibliothèque Nationale, Codex signatus num. 3779. Olim Cluniacensis (?), diende Thuaneus, deinde Colbertinus 612. postea Regius C 3759.6. Foliorum 299 med. (O^m, 30 X O, 25), columnis binis, exaratus sæc. X. Vita Sancti Ambrosii episcopi quod est pridie nonas Aprilis (fol. 153^v-165^r). Auctore Paulino. The text, very carefully written, is complete and closely related to A, although it is in some degree independent of it.

C—Bibliothèque Nationale, Codex signatus num. 2076. Olim cœnobii Deruensis diende Petri Pithœi, diendi Thuaneus, diende Colbertinus 1257, postea Regius C 5775.3. Foliorum 144 med. (O^m, 285 X 0, 23), columnis binis, exaratus sæc. X. Vita Sancti Ambrosii episcopi (fol. 91^v-106^v). Up to Chapter VI, this MS. is very closely related to A and B, but beginning with chapter VI to the end of the text, it varies considerably and becomes very inaccurate in case endings. We frequently came upon readings which were not found in the above mentioned MSS. The text is complete.

D—Bibliothèque Nationale, Codex signatus num. 1771. Olim Colbertinus, deinde Regius C 3752.5. Foliorum 86 med. (O^m, 315 X O^m, 235), lineis plenis, exaratus diuersis manibus sæc. VIII et IX. Vita Sancti Ambrosii episcopi Mediolanesis (fol. 49^r-59^r). Auctore Paulino. The text of this MS. is complete but contains numerous errors. Omissions and interlinear corrections are frequent. Also towards the end of the fourteenth paragraph a different hand can be detected.

The body of the text in all MSS. consulted is continuous, without any division into chapters and no chapter headings. The division into chapters and sections I have taken from the Benedictine Edition, the chapter headings have been taken over from Hurter's edition of the *Vita*.

IV. OCCASION AND DATE

Paulinus[37] makes it known to us in his preface that he undertook the writing of the *Life of Saint Ambrose* to comply with a request of Saint Augustine. Since the latter lived for some time in Milan[38] and frequented the home of Saint Ambrose, he most probably met Paulinus there, then a religious in minor orders. Several years after the death of Saint Ambrose, as we have remarked above, Paulinus betook himself to Africa where he again met Saint Augustine. Knowing of Paulinus's relations with the holy bishop Ambrose and his deep attachment and veneration for his deceased master, Augustine asked him to write the life of Saint Ambrose. He pointed out[39] to him as models three biographies then celebrated in the Latin Church: *The Life of Saint Anthony* by the Blessed Bishop Athanasius,[40] the *Life of Saint Paul* by the Blessed Priest Jerome,[41] and the *Life of Blessed Martin Bishop of Tours*, by Sulpicius Severus,[42] a servant of God.

Finally, yielding to the petition of Saint Augustine,

Paulinus put himself to the task and composed the prologue of the *Vita*, dedicating the work to Saint Augustine. Some of the older ecclesiastical historians seem to believe that the *Life* was written in Milan, but it is certain that Paulinus wrote it in Africa, since he himself said so.[43]

There is nothing in the work itself or in the early writers to supply us with a statement as to the exact date of the composition of the *Vita*. According to Paulinus,[44] he was writing the *Life* when John was Praetorian Prefect, who according to the Theodosian Code[45] held this office in 412–413 and 422.[46] In addition to the above evidence, we read in the *Vita*[47] that Venerius was the successor of Saint Simplicianus, and according to all chronologies, Venerius governed the Church of Milan from AD 400 to 409 and is completely lost to history after 412. Again in the *Vita*[48] we find the statement concerning Saint Felix, "he now governs the Church of Bologna," meaning at the time Paulinus was writing the *Life*. History informs us that Saint Felix was bishop of Bologna from 400 to 430, when he was succeeded by Saint Petronius.[49] Paulinus,[50] furthermore, makes the statement that Zenobius is "now bishop of Florence," who, in fact, held the episcopal see in Florence until either 417 or 424. Antonius, the successor and biographer of Saint Zenobius, informs us that Saint Zenobius died in 424, which was during the pontificate of Pope Innocent I. There is evidently a discrepancy in this statement of Antoninus as history places as the death of Innocent I in 417. If it can be proved that Saint Zenobius died in 417, then the exact date of the composition of the *Vita* would be 412–413 or during John's first term as Praetorian Prefect. But since the date of the death of Saint Zenobius is uncertain, although there is good ground for believing that he actually died in 417, we must be content with ascribing the date of the composition of the *Vita* to the period between 412–422.

V. RELIABILITY OF THE VITA

The *Vita Sancti Ambrosii* belongs to the type of literature known as hagiography, the primary purpose of which is religious, namely, the edification of the reader. This type of literature partakes of the nature of biography, panegyric, and moral instruction. In most of the ancient lives of saints we note that a certain definite method of procedure is followed. Thus in a case of a saint who—like Saint Ambrose—was not a martyr, the "life" is ordinarily divided into three parts: 1. Before the saint's birth: his nationality, his parents, prophesies of his future greatness. 2. His life: childhood, youth, the most important events in his career, his virtues, his miracles. 3. His cultus, and miracles after death. The profession or quality of the saint is also subject to analysis.[51]

Paulinus found this type of literature already fixed, and Saint Augustine[52] pointed out several models for him to follow. From these models he chose especially the *Life of Saint Martin* by Sulpicius Severus. A glance at the structure of the *Vita Sancti Martini* will show how closely he followed this work.[53]

Since the purpose, then, of the hagiographer was primarily to edify his reader and give strength and inspiration to his spiritual life, we must not be surprised to find that many *Vitæ* do not fulfill the requirements of biography in our strictly scientific interpretation of the term. The *Vita* of Paulinus especially fails miserably when judged by these standards. Thus Paulinus pays no heed whatever to chronological details and we can fix the dates of many of the events mentioned in the *Vita* only by consulting Ambrose's own works and other writers and documents of the time. Again, we would never gather from the narrative of Paulinus that Saint Ambrose was one of the really great figures of his age, and one of the last great personalities of the Western Empire. The great bishop's activity in civil affairs is merely touched on incidentally by his biographer and in more than one instance the latter shows but little understanding of his hero's career. Furthermore, as De Labriolle[54] points out, Paulinus does not give us all the information which he should on the religious side of Saint Ambrose. Hence from our point of view, we must admit with Schanz[55] that on the whole the *Vita* is something of a disappointment. However, apart from the defects mentioned, it possesses considerable value inasmuch as it contains many interesting details of Saint Ambrose's private life which have not come down to us in any other work.

In connection with the information furnished by the *Vita* the significant question naturally arises: what credence can be given to the narrative of Paulinus? The integrity of the writer cannot be questioned. He was held in high esteem by Saint Ambrose and Saint Augustine. Two popes, Innocent I and Zosimus, recognized in him a resolute defender of the doctrines of the Church against the heretical teachings of Cœlestius. The straightforward character of the narrative bears witness to his conscientious and sincere effort to fulfill his task to the best of his ability. He was an eyewitness to many of the events narrated, and some of the witnesses whom he cites[56] for events which he has not seen himself are certainly above reproach or question. There is one serious charge, however, which we must make against him: that he did not use Ambrose's own words as much as he should for source material. The letters of Saint Ambrose especially would have been a rich mine of information for him, as those which are extant are for many details in his hero's life. Yet Paulinus cites these letters very infrequently. In one instance, moreover, through lack of understanding or carelessness he misinterprets a very important passage relating to the affair of Thessalonica.[57]

Paulinus is further charged with being over-credulous. This is perhaps true to some extent, but is at least certain that he records honestly what he himself believes to be true. The miracles which he reports on his own authority must be viewed as the evidence of a reliable witness. The character of the miracles which he reports on the authority of others depends on the credence which we can give to his informants. Those miracles which are accepted commonplaces in all early hagiographical literature need not concern us here, as they have been adequately discussed elsewhere.[58]

In conclusion, then, we may say that Paulinus is a conscientious and truthful writer, and that his narrative on the whole may be considered reliable. His chief defects, as a biographer—apart from lack of style—are the many omissions of important events and his failure to appreciate the full significance of Saint Ambrose, especially in his political rôle. The omissions may be explained in part at least by the peculiar nature and purpose of the hagiographer mentioned above. Hence while we admit that the work of Paulinus has serious shortcomings, we must declare that it is a gross injustice to say of it that it is "nothing better that morbid and monkish fiction"[59]

VI: STYLE AND LITERARY SIGNIFICANCE[60]

To be fair in discussing the style of Paulinus it must be brought home to the reader that he was a man of only moderate education and limited ability. Therefore, we search in vain in him for the qualities found in the outstanding writers of the Patristic period. He did not possess originality of thought nor beauty of language. At the very outset,[61] after acknowledging his inferiority to such great men as Athanasius and Jerome in character and literary ability, he prepares us, so to speak, for the panegyrical character of his discourse. For it is only natural that he should pour forth his admiration by relating to posterity the "*gratia uiri*" which belonged to Saint Ambrose, as he writes, from his cradle. In his style, with the exception of the Preface, where we notice an attempt at literary finish, he appears to be a plain and untrained writer. The entire work seems stiff, lacking vivacity and copiousness, and even in places obscure and unattractive. The sentences are in many instances abrupt and loosely connected. Besides being unrhetorical they show neither balance nor finish and are frequently marred by parenthetical statements. There is considerable philosophizing and moralizing, which frequently, being poorly expressed, obscures the entire thought.

A discussion of our author's style should include at least a brief consideration of the rhetorical devices which were so characteristic of the great literary works of the Fourth and Fifth century. We do not, as we have said, meet with such rhetorical display in the *Vita*. In its fifty-six sections, the *Vita* furnishes examples of about twenty-seven figures and many of these, as it would seem, are used entirely without design or deliberation. The greatest number fall under the Figures of Sound, i.e. paranomasia, polyptoton, alliteration, assonance, and parachesis, furnishing us with more than two hundred examples, about eighty of which are assonance. The latter figure seems to be a favorite device with Paulinus. He also shows a fondness for polyptoton of which we find over fifty-five examples, next in rank comes paranomasia, about fifty, but to our surprise, alliteration drops to about thirteen and parachesis to seven.

For examples of alliteration, cf. secs. 1, 23, 7, 33, 43, 45, etc. We find parachesis in sec. 30: *gentes legentes;* sec. 49: *directa... lecta;* sec. 32: *capillus capitis*, et passim.

The devices which would add vivacity and lend dramatic

effect to style are very scanty. Of these parenthesis is the outstanding figure, occurring seven times; then we have six examples of asyndeton, and two each of polysyndeton, litotes, interrogatio, and exclamatio.

Anadiplosis, chiasmus, and epanaphora, special rhetorical devices for indicating emphasis, are but few. The same might be said of the figures of amplification, since we find but five examples of pleonasm and three of arsis and thesis. Some instances of anadiplosis are: sec. 7: *magis magisque; sine pera, sine uirga*, etc.; and of chiasmus, sec. 16: *donatam...reseruabat crescebatque...hominibus;* sec. 40: *ignorantes pium affectum uiri nec qua ratione ita fleret intellegentes.*

The metaphor, so frequent in the writers of the period, is by no means frequent in the *Vita*. Of all the metaphors noted we would say that only eight are worth considering. Of the metaphors the most striking are sec. 1: *qui muri ecclesiarum sunt et eloquentiae fontes;* sec. 41: *deruptis uinculis atque proiecto iugo huiusmodi dominationis;* for others, cf. sec. 8, 21, 31, 39, 41.

Of the devices of parallelism few instances have been noted. This fact confirms our statement above that Paulinus' sentences are unrhetorical, lack balance and finish.

Five examples of hyperbaton and two of antonomasia appear in the work, but the examples noted are not striking.

A noteworthy passage, rich in figurative devices, is sec. 23: *Ego...mysteria*, in which we find striking examples of arsis and thesis, parison, homoioteleuton, isocolon, epanaphora, interrogatio, antithesis, and hypophora.

The *Vita*, in its arrangement, although not strictly chronological, closely resembles the literary form of the Alexandrian biography, which is best seen in the *Lives* of Suetonius.[62] This form of biography aims primarily to portray the character and personal traits of the hero. In all probability, Paulinus's knowledge of this literary form did not come directly from Classical sources but indirectly through the *Lives* of the biographers whom he mentions in the Preface of this *Vita*. This we are inclined to believe because of quite apparent dependence of Paulinus upon his models, especially the *Life of Saint Martin* by Sulpicius Severus. The latter he follows in structure almost absolutely, as is evident from the following:

Vita S. Ambrosii.	*Vita S. Martini.*
Preface, sec. 1–2.	Preface—(Autoris ad Desiderium epistola de libro Vitae B. Martini) and sec. 1 of Liber 1.
Birth, Youth, Early public Career of Saint Ambrose, sec. 3–5.	
Life proper, Deeds, Virtues, and Miracles of Saint Ambrose, sec. 6–52.	Birth, Youth, Early public Career of Saint Martin, sec. 2–4.
Conclusion and Epilogue in the Life of Saint Ambrose, sec. 53–56.	Life proper, Deeds, Virtues, and Miracles of Saint Martin, sec. 5–26.
	Conclusion and Epilogue in the Life of Saint Martin, sec. 27.

What interest and value does the *Vita* have for the literary world? The *Vita S. Ambrosii* has the distinction of being one of our chief sources for Ambrose's life, especially his spiritual life, and reveals many personal traits that we cannot learn from his writings. In the *Vita*[63] we see Ambrose chastising his flesh by labors, by vigils, by fasts, by praying day and night. The beauty of his sympathetic soul is also poured out in the picture of Saint Ambrose weeping with the afflicted and especially with the sinners, causing them

The Life of Saint Ambrose

to weep with him. All this would have been lost had not Paulinus presented it to the reader for imitation[64] and approval of the grace of God which was revealed by his holy and virtuous life.

NOTES

1. Paulinus, Deacon of Milan, must not be confused with Paulinus, the bishop of Nola, who lived between 354 and 431, a contemporary of our author.
2. Bouvy, Paulin de Milan, *Revue Augustinienne*, vol. 1 (1902), 499.
3. Marius Mercator, *Commonitorium super nomine Cœlestii,* cap. I; Saint Augustine, *De Gest. Pelag.*, cap. IX, 23; *et Peccat. Origin.*, cap. XI, 12.
4. Bibliotheca Patrologia Latina, II, 597.
5. Bouvy, Paulin de Milan, *Revue Augustinienne*, vol. I (1902), 499.
6. Epist. LXIII, 82.
7. *Vita Sancti Ambrosii*, Chapter X, paragraph 46.
8. *Vita Sancti Ambrosii*, Chapter IX, paragraph 42.
9. *De Viris Illustribus*, Chapter XVII.
10. *Vita Sancti Ambrosii*, Chapter IX, paragraph 42
11. *Commonitorium super nomine Cœlestii,* cap. I.
12. *De Peccat Origin.*, num. 3, 8, and *Contra duas epist. Pelag.*, lib. II cap. IV, 6.
13. Baronius, Book V. for the year AD 397, parag. 47.
14. *Vita Sancti Ambrosii*, Chapter VIII, paragraph 32–33.
15. *Vita Sancti Ambrosii*, Chapter VIII, paragraph 35.
16. *Vita Sancti Ambrosii*, Chapter IX, paragraph 42.
17. *Vita Sancti Ambrosii*, Chapter IX, paragraph 40.
18. *Vita Sancti Ambrosii*, Chapter IX, paragraph 38–41.
19. *Vita Sancti Ambrosii*, Chapter XI, paragraph 54.
20. *Vita Sancti Ambrosii*, Chapter X, paragraph 51.
21. *Vita Sancti Ambrosii*, Chapter XI, paragraph 54.
22. *De gest. Pelag.*, cap. II, num. 23, and *De peccat. origin.*, cap. XI, num. 12.
23. *Commonitorium super nomine Cœlestii,*, I.
24. In the year AD 416.
25. Saint Augustine, *De peccat. origin.*, cap. III, num. 3.
26. *Commonitorium super nomine Cœlestii,* I.
27. Zosimus, Epist. II.
28. Migne, PP. L. XX, 711–715.
29. *Noris. Hist. Pelag.* lib. I, cap., 12, p. 121, 123.

INTRODUCTION

30. Baronius, for the year AD 418, parag. 11.
31. *De Viris Illustribus,* Chapter XVII: "Paulinus, presbyter, explicit Benedictionibus patriarcharum triplici intelligentiae genere librum satis succincta breuitate compositum. idem etiam, petente Augustino, conscripsit Ambrosii uitam signis florentem, atque doctrinis et meritis apostolorum non imparem. siquidem et Constantius episcopus Germani uitam contexuit, obitumque Paulini Oranius edidit."
32. *Mémoires Eccl.* tom XII, 310.
33. Bardenhewer, vol. IV, 544.
34. Le Commentaire des Bénédictions de Jacob attribue a Paulin de Milan in *Revue Bénédictine*, vol. 32 (1920), 57–63.
35. Bardenhewer, vol. IV, 544.
36. The description of the MSS. with the exception of A, which is from England, are taken from the Bollandist *Catalogus Codicum Hagiographicorum Latinorum Bibliotheca Nationali Parisiensi.*
37. *Vita Sancti Ambrosii,* Chapter I, paragraph 1.
38. *Confessions,* Book V, Chapter 13.
39. *Vita Sancti Ambrosii,* Chapter I, paragraph 1.
40. *Note to the 2019 edition:* See the annotated translation of Athanasius's *Life of Saint Anthony* by Robert T. Meyer, Newman Press.
41. *Note to the 2019 edition:* The work referred to here is Saint Jerome's *Vita* of Saint Paul, the first hermit, not to be confused with the better known Saint Paul of Tarsus whose acts and epistles are included in the canon of Sacred Scripture. An English translation of this work by Saint Jerome may be found in the *Select Library of Nicene and Post-Nicene Fathers of the Christian Church, Second Series, Volume VI: Saint Jerome: Letters and Selected Works.*
42. *Note to the 2019 edition:* See the English translation of Sulpicius Severus's *Life of Saint Martin* edited by Philip Burton.
43. *Vita Sancti Ambrosii,* Chapter X, paragraph 51; Chapter XI, paragraph 54
44. *Vita Sancti Ambrosii,* Chapter VIII, paragraph 31.
45. Gothofredus, *Prosopographia Codicis Theodos.*, 61.
46. John entered office on June 6, 412, and his first term expired on June 12, 413. He was again given this office in 422, his term commencing on July 11 of that year. Cf Pauly-Wissowa, *Realencyclopädie,* vol. IX, 1744.
47. *Vita Sancti Ambrosii,* Chapter X, paragraph 46.
48. *Vita Sancti Ambrosii,* Chapter X, paragraph 46.
49. Some of these dates are discussed by Van Ortroy, Les Vies Greques de S. Ambroise, 7–8.

50. *Vita Sancti Ambrosii,* Chapter X, paragraph 50.
51. Delehaye, H., *Legends of the Saints,* 98.
52. *Vita Sancti Ambrosii,* Chapter I, paragraph 1.
53. See the section on Style and Literary Significance in the introduction to the present volume.
54. Labriolle, *Saint Ambroise,* 2–3.
55. *Römische Literaturgeschichte,* Vol. VIII, 286.
56. Eye-witnesses cited by Paulinus include: Saint Marcellina, (See the present volume Chapter I, Paragraph 1; Saint Simplicianus and Saint Venerius, Chapter X, Paragraph 46; Saint Felix, bishop of Bologna, Chapter X, Paragraph 46; Saint Zenobius, bishop of Florence, Chapter X, Paragraph 47; Saint Bassianus, bishop of Lodi, Chapter X, Paragraph 47; Saint Honoratus, bishop of Vercelli, Chapter X, Paragraph 47.
57. Cf. Koch, H., in *Historisches Jahrbuch,* vol. XXVIII (1907), 267–269.
58. Delehaye, H., *The Legends of the Saints,* 50–59.
59. Farrar, *Lives of the Fathers,* Vol. II, 89.
60. *Note to the 2019 edition:* Two sections of Sr. Mary Kaniecka's original introduction relating to technical aspects of the vocabulary and syntax of Paulinus's Latin text have been left out here.
61. *Vita Sancti Ambrosii,* Book I, Chapter 1.
62. Leo, F., *Die Griechische-Römische Biographie,* 11–16.
63. *Vita Sancti Ambrosii,* Paragraph 38–42.
64. *Vita Sancti Ambrosii,* Paragraph 55.

THE LIFE OF SAINT AMBROSE, BISHOP OF MILAN[1]

WRITTEN BY HIS SECRETARY PAULINUS TO BLESSED AUGUSTINE

CHAPTER I
THE AUTHOR'S PREFACE.

1. You urge, reverend father Augustine, that just as those blessed men, the Bishop Athanasius and the priest Jerome described with their pens the lives of Saints Paul and Anthony who lived in the desert, just as also Severus,[2] a servant of God, composed in an elegant language the life of reverend Martin, Bishop of the church of Tours, so too, I describe with my pen the life of blessed Ambrose, bishop of the church of Milan. But just as I realize that I am inferior to such men in worth, who are the bulwarks of the churches and fountains of eloquence, so also do I realize that I am unequal to them in power of expression. However, since I think it would be without reason to refuse what you bid, whatever I have learned from those most trustworthy who served him before me and especially his own sister, the reverend Marcellina,[3] or whatever I myself have seen, when I was in his service, or what I have learned from those who related that they had seen him after his death in different provinces, or what was written to him when it was still unknown that he had died. All this, assisted by your prayers and by the worth of so great a man, I shall describe—

although in unadorned language—briefly and summarily, so that even if the language offend the mind of the reader, yet its brevity may encourage him to read it. And I shall not obscure the truth with florid words, lest while the writer seek the pomp of elegant diction, the reader, whom it does not befit to look for the trappings of pomp of expression more than the virtue of deeds and the grace of the Holy Spirit, miss the knowledge of so great virtues. For we may know that travelers regard as more pleasing the water that trickles in a feeble rill when perchance they are thirsty, than the streams of a gushing fountain, whose plenty they cannot find at the time of their thirst. And barley bread is wont to be sweet even to those who are accustomed to belch up the abundance of their daily banquet with its countless courses of dishes. And the wild plants are accustomed to please even those who admire charming gardens.

2. On this account, I beseech you all in whose hands this book will fall, to believe that what we say is true. And let no one think that I have put down anything which lacks truth, through the bias of love, since indeed it is better to say nothing at all than to set forth something that is false, when we know that *we shall render an account of all our words.*[4] And I should not doubt, although all things are not known by all, that yet various things are known by various people, and that those facts are known to some, which even I myself was not able to hear or see. Therefore, I shall take up the beginning of the narrative from the day of his birth, so that the divine grace which belonged to the man from his cradle may be well known.

NOTES

1. The exact title, if any, given by Paulinus to his *Life of Saint Ambrose* is difficult to determine. The titles given in the four MSS. consulted somewhat differ, but the identical element in them is the *"Vita Sancti Ambrosii Episcopi."* We have adopted the title: *"Vita*

Sancti Ambrosii Mediolanensis Episcopi A Paulino Eius Notario Ad Beatum Augustinum Conscripta," the heading used by Migne in his edition.

2. Sulpicius Severus, a descendant of a noble family of Aquitaine, was born about AD 363. He embraced the law, but after the death of his wife retired into solitude through the influence of Saint Martin of Tours, as some think, and spent the rest of his life in literary labors and works of piety. Whether he was a priest is uncertain, as no details of his priestly activities have come down to us. His death occurred between 410–420.

3. Saint Marcellina, the only sister of Saint Ambrose, was born about AD 330, probably at Trier, where her father abode as Prætorian Prefect of the Gauls. After his death the family removed to Rome, and there Marcellina consecrated her life to God by taking the vow of virginity. On that occasion Pope Liberius delivered a discourse which Saint Ambrose recorded in his *De Virginibus.* He also addressed to her three of his most important letters: Epistle XX, describing his conflict with Justina and her son, the younger Valentinian; Epistle XXII, announcing the discoveries of the bodies of Saints Gervase and Protase; and Epistle XLI, reporting a sermon in which he had reproved Theodosius on the subject of the punishment inflicted by the emperor on some Christians who had burned a Jewish synagogue. Ambrose, in his discourse on the death of his brother Satyrus, speaks of the warm family affection by which the three were bound and of his sister's great grief. About 374 when Saint Ambrose had become Bishop of Milan, he summoned his sister thither in whom he found a zealous assistant in promoting the ascetic life among the virgins in Milan. While in Milan, Paulinus learned from Marcellina the details of Saint Ambrose's life. Saint Marcellina survived her brother and died about 398. She was buried in the crypt of the Ambrosian Basilica. Her feast is celebrated on July 17. Cf. Smith and Wace, *Dictionary of Christian Biography,* III, 844; *Catholic Encyclopedia* IX, 637.

4. Matthew 12:36.

CHAPTER II

BIRTH, YOUTH, AND EARLY PUBLIC CAREER OF SAINT AMBROSE.

3. Ambrose, then, was born while his father, Ambrose,[1] was engaged in the administration of the Prefectureship

of the Gallic provinces.² And when he, an infant, placed in a cradle within the courtyard of the governor's residence was sleeping with open mouth, suddenly a swarm of bees came and covered his face and lips in such a way that they kept entering and coming forth alternately. The father, who was walking near by with his wife³ and daughter, fearing lest the bees might be driven away by the servant who had undertaken the task of feeding the baby, kept her back—for she was alarmed lest they injure the child—and with fatherly affection waited to see with what end this miracle would terminate. And sometime later flying out they rose to such a height into the air that they could not be seen at all by human eyes. Terrified by this event the father said: "If this little child shall live, he shall be something great." For at that time the Lord in the infancy of His servant was working for the fulfillment of what has been written: *Good works are as a honeycomb*.⁴ For that swarm of bees was generating for us the honeycombs of his writings which were to announce the gifts of heaven and raise the minds of men from earthly things to heaven.

4. Afterwards, in fact, when he had grown and settled in the city of Rome with his widowed mother and sister—who had already professed virginity together with another girl, whose sister Candida⁵ herself also is of the same profession and is now an old woman in Carthage—when he saw the hands of bishops kissed by a member of the household, he was himself wont to offer his right hand playfully to his sister or mother, saying that this should also be done to him by her because he would be a bishop. For the Holy Spirit spoke in him Who was nurturing him for the episcopacy, but she repelled him on the ground that he was a youth and knew not what he said.

5. And when after being instructed in the liberal disciplines⁶ he had departed from the city and had taken

Chapter II

up his profession in the court of the Prætorian Prefect, he pleaded his cases so brilliantly that he was chosen by the Illlustrious[7] Probus,[8] then Prætorian Prefect, to act as his adviser. After this he received the dignity of the consulship[9] so that he should rule over the provinces of Liguria and Æmilia,[10] and he came to Milan.

NOTES

1. The father of Saint Ambrose was a Roman of the highest rank, and at the time of Saint Ambrose's birth was the *Præfectus Galliarum* ruling the present territories of France, Britain and Spain, together with Tingitana in Africa. It was one of the four great præfectures of the empire, as will be explained below, and the highest office entrusted to a subject. It is not known in which of the principal cities of this province the prefect resided when his son Ambrose was born, but since Treves or Trier was the seat of the *præfectus*, most probably it was here that Saint Ambrose was born. About the year 354 the father died, and the rest of the family removed to Rome. Cf. Smith and Wace, *Dictionary of Christian Biography,* I, 91.
2. Diocletian instituted sweeping changes in the administration of the empire. Constantine followed his lead and established a system of civil administration, at the head of which stood four Prætorian Prefects, though unlike the *præfectus prætorio* of Augustus, who was a military officer. Each of these men was styled, respectively: Prætorian Prefect of the East, of Illyricum, of Italy, and of the Gauls. It was the privilege of the *præfectus* to nominate to the emperor the governors of the provinces into which his *præfectura* was divided, to supervise the conduct of these governors, to remove them from office if he deemed it advisable. He had absolute judiciary powers and had complete control of imperial finances in his *præfectura*. The term of office is said to have been short. The prefecture of the Gauls included the following provinces: Hispania, Aquitania, Gallia Narbonensis, Lugdunensis, Belgica, Germania inferior et superior, Britania and Mauretania in Africa. The seat of the *præfectus Galliarum* was Treves or Trier, in modern Germany. Cf. Greenidge, *Student's Gibbon,* I, 158–161.
3. We know very little about Ambrose's mother except that on the death of her husband she moved to Rome.
4. Proverbs 16:24.
5. Nothing further is known concerning the life of Candida. G. Clausse in his *Basiliques et Mosaiques Chrétiennes* (Paris, 1898),

399, speaks in connection with the Ambrosian Basilica of three medallions: the first a female head bearing the subscription *Sca Marcellina;* the second, a male head, bearing the name *S. Satyrus;* and the third, a female head, with the subscription *Sca Candida.* This latter may refer to the Candida above mentioned.

6. The Liberal Disciplines, according to Aristotle (*Politics,* VIII, 1), are the proper studies for freeman seeking intellectual and moral excellence in general, rather than the studies of immediate practical value. He draws a clear distinction between a liberal and a technical education.

    The liberal disciplines of the Greeks became the recognized ground-work for the education of the Romans, known among them as *artes liberales, studia liberalia, liberales disciplinae,* or *liberales scientiae.* Grammar, dialects, rhetoric, geometry, arithmetic, astrology, music, medicine and architecture were the nine disciplines as named by Varro. In the early empire the arts, probably seven, due to Alexandrian influence, became closely coördinated as a body of school instruction, known as encyclical education.

    Among the Christians, especially in the Western Church, there was a strong spirit of antagonism towards the arts at first, but gradually this feeling changed to active encouragement of the liberal disciplines on the ground that they ministered to higher spiritual truth. This transition is especially noticed in the writings of Saint Augustine, cf. *De Doctrina Christiana.* Although the latter considered Varro as his authority in the matters pertaining to the history of the liberal arts, he does not adhere to Varro's number of disciplines and instead of nine he enumerates seven. In Martianus Capella of Carthage (*De Nuptiis Philologiæ et Mercurii*) we find for the first time an express limitation of the arts to seven. He excludes medicine and architecture as being utilitarian. Boethius next divides them into quadrivium: arithmetic, geometry, music, astronomy and trivium: grammar, rhetoric and dialects. And so all subsequent writers, as Cassiodorus, Isidore of Seville, Alcuin, and Rabanus Maurus call them *septem artes liberales,* which are the ancient *artes liberales* Christianized. Cf. *Catholic Encyclopedia* I, 760–765; Harper's *Dictionary of Classical Literature and Antiquities,* 952–953.

7. *Illustres* (Illustrious), *Spectabiles* (Respectable), and *Clarissimi* (Honorable) were the titles given to magistrates and officials by Diocletian and Constantine, *Illustres* being considered the highest of the three. From the time of Valentinian I, *Illustres* became an official title of the consuls, of the chief *præfecti* or ministers, and of the commander-in-chief of the army. Eventually, however, this title was

Chapter II

extended to less important officials and even to pensionaries from the order of *Spectabiles*. The great privilege of the *Illustres* was that in criminal cases they were tried by none save the emperor or his deputy. A further privilege of delegating procurators to represent them in the courts also belonged to the *Illustres*. *Spectabiles* was a title given to all members of the senate, and to all those who from this body were selected to govern the provinces.

The prefectures were governed by *illustres præfecti prætorio*, the dioceses by *Spectabiles vicarii* and the provinces by *Clarissimi consulares*. Cf. Greenidge, *Student's Gibbon* I, 161 note, also *Abbot's Political Institutions*, 156–157; Hodgkin, *Italy and Her Invaders*, Volume I, Book 1, 604–617.

8. Petronius Probus gained distinction and prestige by becoming allied by marriage to the great Anician *gens*, known for its wealth, official distinction, and devotion to Christianity. He was consul with Gratian in AD 371, and held the office of Prætorian Prefect of Italy, Illyricum, the Gauls, and Africa four times. In 358 he was pro-consul of Africa and next he was Prefect of Italy, which office he held until the death of Valentinian or until 374. Later in 383–384 he was Prætorian Prefect and after the murder of Gratian in 383 he acted as regent to Valentinian II. It was during his tenure of office that he chose Ambrose to be one of his council, later appointing him governor of Liguria and Æmilia with the rank of consul. He died in 394 at the age of sixty, after having received baptism. Cf. Smith and Wace, *Dictionary of Christian Biography*, IV, 481.

9. During the republican period the term consular rank was applied only to persons holding the consulship, while under the empire it was a mere title and we find officers thus entitled who never actually became consuls. It might be said that the title became almost equivalent to that of an honorary consul. Very frequently persons after their consulship became generals of the army in the provinces, hence this title of "Consular rank" was given them. Later *consularis* became an established title of the governors entrusted with the administration of imperial provinces. Thus, in the second century AD this title always denotes a governor who actually held the office of a consul or received the rank from the emperor *per codicillos*, but by the fourth century it was a mere title of a particular class of provincial governors. Cf. Smith's *Dictionary of Greek and Roman Antiquities*. 537–538.

10. Liguria, a district of Italy, constituted the ninth region in the division made by Augustus. All through the empire the boundaries of Liguria remained unchanged, but during the reign of Constantine the province of Cottian Alps was incorporated with Liguria and the

name was changed to Alpes Cottiae, the name Liguria being then transferred to the eleventh region, or Gallia Transpadana. At this time—that is, when Ambrose received the consular rank—Liguria corresponded to Northern Piedmont and part of Western Lombardy.

Æmilia retained its ancient name which it received from the Via Æmilia constructed by M. Æmilius Lipidus. It was a district of about 150 miles and marks the course of the Po river on its southern bank. Both provinces were under one governor, Milan being the seat of government. Cf. Smith, *Dictionary of Greek and Roman Geography* II, 183-189; Baedeker, K., *Northern Italy,* 63–64, 297–299.

CHAPTER III

HE IS ELECTED BISHOP OF MILAN, NOT WITHOUT THE WILL OF GOD. HE TRIES TO EVADE BUT IN VAIN. HIS ELECTION IS CONFIRMED BY MIRACLES.

6. At the same time, Auxentius[1] being dead, a bishop of the Arian heresy who, after Dionysius[2] the confessor[3] of blessed memory had been sent into exile, held possession of the Church. Ambrose proceeded to the church, since the people in seeking a bishop were rising to revolt and it was his care to quell sedition lest the people of the city should be turned to do harm to themselves. And there while he was addressing the populace, a voice of a child is said to have suddenly cried out among the people: "Ambrose bishop!" At the sound of this voice the mouths of all the people were changed, all crying: "Ambrose bishop!" Thus those who disagreed most violently before, because both the Arians and the Catholics wished the other party to be defeated and a bishop of their own to be appointed, suddenly insisted on this one man with miraculous and incredible harmony.

7. When he noticed this, leaving the church, he had a tribunal prepared for himself—naturally about to become a bishop he mounted higher things. Then contrary to his

Chapter III

custom he ordered tortures to be applied to certain persons. Although he was doing this, the people nevertheless kept shouting: "Your sin be upon us." But those people then shouted not in the manner of the Jews, for the latter by their words shed the blood of the Lord, saying: *"His blood be upon us,"*[4] but the former knowing that he was a catechumen,[5] with the voice of faith assured him the forgiveness of all sins through the grace of baptism. Then returning home disturbed he wished to declare himself a philosopher. But he was to be a true philosopher of Christ, because despising worldly pomp he was about to follow the footsteps of the Fisherman, who united the people to Christ not by the ornaments of expression but by artless speech and by the doctrine of the true faith—being sent without wallet, without staff, they converted even the philosophers themselves. When he was prevented from doing this, he had common women come publicly to him for this purpose only—that when they were seen, the purpose of the people might be changed. But the people kept shouting more and more: "Your sin be upon us."

8. But when he saw that he could not carry out his resolution, he prepared himself for flight, leaving the city at midnight. Since he intended to proceed to Ticinum,[6] in the morning he was found at the gate of the city of Milan which is called Roman.[7] For God, Who was preparing a bulwark for his Catholic Church against its enemies and erecting a tower of David against the face of Damascus, that is, the faithlessness of the heretics, prevented his flight. After he was found and while he was being guarded by the people, a relation was sent to the most kind emperor then Valentinian,[8] who heard with greatest joy that the judges sent out by him were sought for the episcopacy. Probus the Prefect also rejoiced because his word was being fulfilled in Ambrose, for he had said to him when he was giving him a

commission on setting out—as is the custom—"Go, act not as judge but as bishop."

9. And so while the relation was pending he again prepared for flight and hid himself for some time on the estate of a certain Honorable Leontius. But when the answer was made to the relation, he was betrayed by the same Leontius. For the lieutenant of the Prætorian Prefect had received orders that he should insist on carrying out the matter, and since he wished to fulfill what he had been enjoined upon him, having published and edict he warned all, saying that if they wished to look to themselves and their welfare, they should give up the man. And so when being handed over and brought to Milan, he recognized the will of God toward him and that he could not resist longer, he demanded that he should not be baptized save by a Catholic bishop, for he carefully guarded against the heresy of the Arians. And so on being baptized he is said to have fulfilled all the ecclesiastical offices and on the eighth day was consecrated bishop with the greatest favor and joy of all. Now a few years after his ordination he proceeded to the city of Rome, that is, to his estate and there found in his home with his sister—just as when he had left—the holy virgin of whom we have spoken above and to whom he was accustomed to hold out his hand, his mother having since died. And when she kissed his hand he said to her, smiling: "Behold, as I used to tell you, you are kissing the hand of a bishop."

10. At the same time when he was invited to the home of a very noble lady across the Tiber to offer the Holy Sacrifice in her house, a certain woman, caretaker of baths who lay in bed paralyzed, having heard that a bishop of the Lord was there, had herself carried in a litter to the same house to which he had come on invitation and touched his garments as he prayed and placed his hands upon her.

Chapter III

When she kissed them eagerly, her health was restored immediately and she began to walk, so that the words of our Lord which were said to His Apostles were fulfilled: *"You shall do even greater things, believing in my name."*[9] Yet just as this miraculous cure was wonderful, so also was it not kept secret, for in this same district many years after, while living in the city, I learned this on the authority of holy men.

11. But when he had come to Sirmium[10] to consecrate Anemius[11] as bishop, he was nearly driven from the church by the power of Justina,[12] the empress at the time, and by a multitude which had been gathered together. They intended that there might be no consecration by Ambrose but that an Arian bishop might be consecrated by the heretics in that very church. And when Ambrose had taken his place on the tribunal, caring nothing for the turmoil which was being stirred up by a woman, one of the Arian maidens, more imprudent than the rest, after ascending the tribunal and seizing the garment of the bishop, since she wished to drag him to a group of women so that he might be beaten by them and driven from the church, heard these words—as he himself was wont to relate: "Even if I am unworthy of so great an episcopal office, yet it does not become you or your profession to lay hands on any bishop whatsoever. Wherefore, you should fear the judgment of God lest something may happen to you." The event confirmed his words. On the following day he conducted her dead to the grave repaying kindness for insult. And this event threw no little fear in his opponents and brought great peace to the Catholic Church at the consecration of the bishop.

NOTES

1. In 355, after the banishment of Dionysius, bishop of Milan, Auxentius was made bishop of that see through Arian intrigue. He

was a native of Cappadocia, filled with bitter hatred of the Catholic faith and a violent persecutor of his orthodox subjects. Saint Hilary of Poitiers publicly accused him at Milan in 364 and consequently, in a disputation held at that city by order of the emperor, Valentinian, he was convicted of error. His submission was only apparent, however, and he remained powerful enough to compel the departure of Saint Hilary from Milan. Saint Athanasius in a synod at Rome in 369 procured his condemnation by Pope Damasus. Auxentius, nevertheless, retained possession of his see until his death in 374. He held the see of Milan for nearly twenty years. He was succeeded by Saint Ambrose. Cf. *Catholic Encyclopedia,* I, 384.

2. Saint Dionysius was the bishop of Milan from 346 until his banishment by the Arian emperor Constantius in 355. He never returned from exile, as two years after the banishment he died in Asia, where he acquired a high reputation for sanctity. In his sermon against Auxentius, Saint Ambrose calls his see, "an inheritance of Dionysius in his Letter LXIII in which he writes concerning the virtues required of a bishop.

    Saint Ambrose received his body in Milan with honor, where it was sent under the sanction of Saint Basil and Saint Aurelius, the local bishop. Cf. Smith and Wace, *Dictionary of Christian Biography,* I, 852; *Catholic Encyclopedia,* I, 384; X, 300.

3. The word *confessor* is used by the Christians as a title of honor given to those who confessed Christ publicly in the times of persecution, and remained faithful to their confession until the end. *Confessor* in the fourth century signified those Christians who were remarkable for their virtues and knowledge, confessing the faith of Christ by the practice of the most heroic virtues, by their preaching and writings. Cf. *Thesaurus Linguæ Latinæ,* IV, 191, 81 ff.; *Catholic Encyclopedia,* IV, 215.

4. Matthew 27:25.

5. A catechumen is a person undergoing a course of preparation prior to reception into the Church. This course consisted of preliminary instructions, through which the convert became acquainted with the doctrines of the Church and divine law. Even in the times of the Apostles we read of such instructions, and we find the mention of catechist and catechumen. However, just what the regulations were it is difficult to determine. By the end of the second century the catechumenate was in force in all its main lines, while in the third and fourth centuries we find the catechumenate flourishing in its full form. Concerning the division of the catechumens and for a further treatment of the question, cf. *Catholic Encyclopedia,* III, 430–432.

6. Ticinum, a city of Gallia Transpadania, is situated on the river

Chapter III

Ticinus in a fertile plain connected at present with Milan by the Naviglio Canal. We find the earliest mention of Ticinum in history by Tacitus (*Annals,* III, 5) on the occasion of the death of Drusus, father of Germanicus. After this it is frequently mentioned during the civil wars. Already under the Roman Republic it became a municipal town and after the fall of the Empire it rose to the position it subsequently occupied. After being devastated in 422 by Attila, it was rebuilt by Theodoric. In 744, after being taken by Charlemagne, the name was changed to Papia or modern Pavia. We find no remains of antiquity in modern Pavia except a few sarcophagi and inscriptions. Cf. Smith, *Dictionary of Greek and Roman Geography* II, 1205–1206; *Catholic Encyclopedia,* XI, 592.

7. Porta Romana is situated between Corso di Porta Romana and Corso Lodi. It opens up northwest to Corso di Porta Romana, northeast to Bast de Romana, southeast to Corso Lodi, and west to Bast di Porta Vigentina. Cf. Baedeker, *Northern Italy,* facing 89.

8. *Note to the 2019 edition:* Valentinian I was declared emperor by the army following the death of Jovian in AD 364. He appointed his brother Valens as co-emperor to rule the east while he ruled the west. Known as an effective emperor and skillful defender of the frontiers, he named his nine year-old son Gratian as co-emperor along with Valens in AD 368. Though Valens became known as a strong supporter of the Arians, Valentinian gravitated toward orthodoxy. He was more tolerant of paganism than his successors, however, and supported Auxentius, the Arian predecessor of Ambrose as bishop of Milan. Valentinian I reigned through 375 when he suddenly died of a stroke after an angry exchange with a Sarmatian envoy. See Catholic Encyclopedia (1912) Volume 15, "Valentinian I". See also *Ecclesiastical History* of Sozomen, Book VI, Chapter 36.

9. John 14:12.

10. Sirmium or modern Mitrovitz, was an important city in the southeastern part of Lower Pannonia. Since the time Sirmium was made the chief depôt of military stores it kept growing until it became an outstanding city in Pannonia. Whether it ever became a Roman colony is not known. We still find extensive ruins of Sirmium about the modern town of Mitrovitz. Cf. Smith, *Dictionary of Greek and Roman Geography,* II, 1014. *Note to the 2019 edition:* Priscus mentions that the city was captured by Attila. See T*he Fragmentary History of Priscus*, page 58.

11. Anemius is mentioned in the *Gesta Concilii Aquileiensis contra Palladium et Secundianum Hæreticos*, as being one of the many bishops who composed the above mentioned Council of Aquileia. Nothing else seems to be known of him. Cf. Ambrose, Epistle 8.

12. Justina, an Arian, was the wife of Valentinian I. After the death of Valentinian, their son Valentinian II, 6 years old, his brother Gratian and his uncle Valens, jointly ruled the empire. Justina, taking advantage of the influence which her position as mother of the young emperor gave her, tried earnestly to advance the interests of the Arian sect. This brought her into collision with Saint Ambrose. About AD 380 Saint Ambrose was summoned to Sirmium to take part in the consecration of Anemius as bishop of that see. This event brought about the first contest between Justina and the holy bishop. Cf. Smith and Wace, *Dictionary of Christian Biography,* III, 537.

CHAPTER IV

THE EMPRESS JUSTINA PERSECUTES THE HOLY BISHOP.

12. And so after a Catholic bishop was consecrated, he returned to Milan and there withstood countless insidious attacks of the above mentioned woman Justina who, by bestowing offices and honors, aroused the people against the holy man. And the weak were deceived by such promises, for she promised tribuneships and various other offices of authority to those who would drag him from the church and lead him into exile. While many tried this but through the protection of God were not strong enough to accomplish it, one more wretched than the rest, Euthymius by name, was incited to such a pitch of fury that he bought a house for himself near the church and in it placed a wagon in order that he might the more easily seize him and, having placed him in the cart, carry him into exile. *But his iniquity came down upon his own head,*[1] for a year from that very day on which he planned to seize him, he himself, placed in the same cart, was sent from the same house into exile, reflecting that this had been turned upon him by the just judgment of God, that he was being taken into exile on that very cart which he himself had prepared for the bishop. And the bishop offered him no little consolation by giving him

Chapter IV

expenses and other things which were necessary.

13. But this acknowledgement on the part of the man checked neither the fury of the woman nor the folly of the crazed Arians, for roused with greater madness, they endeavored to break into the Portian Basilica,[2] even an army under arms was sent to guard the doors of the church that no one might dare to enter the Catholic church. But the Lord, who is wont to grant triumphs to His Church over its adversaries, moved the hearts of the soldiers to the defense of His church, so that turning their shields, they guarded the doors of the church, not permitting anyone to go out but also not preventing the Catholic people from entering the church. But not even this could suffice for the soldiers who had been sent, for they too acclaimed the Catholic faith along with the people.[3] At this time antiphons, hymns, and vigils began first to be practiced in the church of Milan.[4] The devotion to this practice continues even to this very day not only in the same church but almost through all the provinces of the West.

NOTES

1. Psalms 7:17.
2. The Portian Basilica was a church outside the walls of Milan, mentioned by Saint Ambrose himself in Letter XX, where he tells his sister Marcellina that the Arians no longer demanded the Portian Basilica but the new basilica which is within the walls. In this letter he describes to her how the basilica had been occupied by soldiers, who, however, fraternized with the Catholics. He also gives a sketch of his sermon on that occasion, comparing the trials of the people to those of Job.
3. *Note to the 2019 edition:* A detailed account of this incident at the Portian basilica, including numerous references to Ambrose's letters, may be found in Lenox-Conyngham's article "The Topography of the Basilica Conflict of AD 385/6 in Milan," in *Historia: Zeitschrift für Alte Geschicte,* 1982.
4. Ambrose, seeing that the spirits of the people closed in the basilica were beginning to flag, tried to occupy their minds by frequent

psalmody. Being a poet as well as an orator, he composed in a simple but sweet melody aspirations of the human soul after God and ordered the depressed congregation to sing them antiphonically. Ambrose, by this introduction of the hymns into the liturgical service, enriched and developed it according to the manner of the oriental custom. This custom spread from Milan through all the Western Churches. There was much controversy as to what hymns Saint Ambrose actually composed and four hymns: *Aeterne rerum Conditor, Deus Creator omnium, iam surgit hora tertia, Veni Redemptor gentium* are vouched for as authentic by historical evidence and especially by the testimony of Saint Augustine, *Confessions,* Book IX, Chapter 7.

These hymns are composed in iambic diameters and arranged in strophes of four verses each. The meter is scrupulously correct and the diction, lucid and simple, is elevated and grave.

It has been believed that in 387, on the occasion of the baptism of Saint Augustine by Saint Ambrose, both sang alternately the canticle, *Te Deum Laudamus*. However, it is certain now that this hymn is not the work of Saint Ambrose and Saint Augustine, but that it was a well-known hymn in the early part of the sixth century. Cf. *Catholic Encyclopedia*. I, 392; Smith and Wace, *Dictionary of Christian Biography,* I, 95.

CHAPTER V

HE FINDS THE BODIES OF THE HOLY MARTYRS GERVASE AND PROTASE, ON WHICH OCCASION DEVILS ARE DRIVEN FROM THE BODIES OF THE POSSESSED. THE BLINDNESS AND IMPUDENCE OF THE ARIANS.

14. At this same time the holy martyrs Protase and Gervase[1] revealed themselves to the Bishop. For they had been placed in the basilica in which today are the bodies of the martyrs Nabor and Felix. And the holy martyrs Nabor and Felix were being visited very frequently, but just as the names of the holy martyrs Gervase and Protase were unknown, so also were their burial places, so much so that all walked over their graves who wished to come to the grates by which the sepulchers of the holy martyrs Nabor and Felix[2]

were protected from injury. But when the bodies of the holy martyrs were taken out and placed on biers, thereupon the diseases of many were shown to have been cured. Even a blind man, Serverus[3] by name, who to the present day devoutly serves in that same basilica which is called the Ambrosian[4] and into which the bodies of the martyrs were carried, as soon as he touched the clothing of the martyrs, immediately received his sight. Bodies, also, possessed by unclean spirits were cured and returned home with the greatest gratitude. And as the faith of the Catholic Church increased by these blessings effected through the martyrs, so did the heresy of the Arians diminish.

15. Finally, from this time, the persecution which was aroused by the fury of Justina, that the bishop might be driven from the church, began to subside. However, in the palace a great number of Arians siding with Justina scoffed at so great a grace of God which the Lord Jesus deigned to confer upon the Catholic Church through the merits of His martyrs, and they said that the venerable man, Ambrose, by means of money had procured men to say falsely that they were troubled by unclean spirits and to assert that they were tortured by him just as also by the martyrs. But the Arians uttered this with the words of the Jews—indeed being very like them—for the latter said of the Lord that *He drove out devils in the name of Beelzebub, the prince of devils.*[5] The former said of the martyrs and of the bishop of the Lord, that not by the grace of God which operated through them were the unclean spirits driven out, but that after receiving money, they said falsely that they were tortured. For the devils called out: "We know you are martyrs," and the Arians said: "We do not know that you are martyrs." Now we read this in the Gospel also, when the devils spoke to the Lord Jesus: *"We know You, that You are the Son of God."*[6] and the Jews said: *"But as to this man we know not whence*

He is."[7] But here is understood not the testimony of the devils, but their confession, wherefore the more wretched are the Arians and the Jews that they should deny what the devils confess.

16. But God who is wont to increase the grace of His Church, did not long permit His Saints to be reviled by the faithless. So one of this number, suddenly possessed by an unclean spirit, began to shout that those who denied the martyrs or who did not believe in the unity of the Trinity—which Ambrose teaches—were being tortured as he himself was. But they, disturbed by these words, who should have been converted and done penance worthy of such a confession, immersed the man in a pond and killed him, adding murder to their unbelief, for a deserving fate drove them to this end. Yet Saint Ambrose, having become a man of greater humility as a bishop, preserved the grace given him by the Lord and increased daily in his faith and love before the eyes of God and men.

17. At this same time there was a certain man of the Arian heresy, a very keen polemicist and hardened and inconvertible to the Catholic faith. He, being in the church while the bishop was preaching saw, as he himself afterwards said, an angel speaking into the ears of the bishop as he preached, so that the bishop seemed to be proclaiming the words of the angel to the people. Being converted at this sight, he himself began to defend the faith which he was wont to attack.

18. There were also at that time two chamberlains of the emperor Gratian, members of the Arian heresy, who proposed a question for the bishop to discuss and, to hear it discussed, promised to be present at the Portian Basilica the next day, for it was a question concerning the Incarnation of the Lord. But on the next day these miserable men filled with swollen pride and unmindful of their promise,

Chapter V

despising God in the person of his bishop and taking no consideration of the injustice done of the waiting people, unmindful also of the words of the Lord that *"he that shall scandalize one of these little ones ought to have a mill stone hanged about his neck and be drowned in the depth of the sea,"*[8] mounting a traveling carriage as if for a drive, they left the city while the bishop waited and the people were in the church. And I shudder as I tell what the outcome of this insolence was: for being hurled suddenly from the carriage they lost their lives and their bodies were given over for burial. But Saint Ambrose, since he did not know what had happened and was no longer able to hold the people, rising before the tribunal began a sermon on the very question which had been proposed, saying: "Brethren, I desire my debt to be paid, but I do not find my creditors of yesterday," and so forth, as it is written in the book which is entitled: "On the Incarnation of the Lord."[9]

NOTES

1. Saints Gervase and Protase, brothers, sons of Vitalis and Valeria, suffered martyrdom in Milan either under Nero or Domitian. About AD 300, the memory of these martyrs faded away and Saint Augustine tells us in his *Confessions* (Book IX, Chapter 7), in the *City of God* (Book XXII, Chapter 8), and in Sermon 286, *In natal. SS. MM. Gervasius and Protasius* and in 318, that God revealed to Saint Ambrose by a vision in a dream the place where their bodies lay. Concerning the vision, the subsequent discovery of the relics, and the accompanying miracles, Saint Ambrose wrote to his sister Marcellina (Letter XXII). Cf. Smith and Wace, *Dictionary of Christian Biography,* II, 666–667.
2. Saints Nabor and Felix owe their celebrity in the universal Church to Saint Ambrose who, about a century after their martyrdom, solemnly translated and enshrined their bodies in Milan. A church, which today bears the name of Saint Francis, was built over their tomb and here they are honored to this day. It is believed that they suffered about 304 in Milan under Maximian Hercules. Their feast is celebrated July 12. Cf. Boll. *Acta* SS. 12 July III, 291; Smith and Wace, *Dictionary of Christian Biography,* IV, 1. Cf. also Letter XX

The Life of Saint Ambrose

of Saint Ambrose in which he mentions the burial places of these martyrs.

3. Severus was a citizen of Milan, well known to the whole town. He had been a butcher but was obliged, by the loss of his sight, to give up his trade. This miracle of Severus regaining his sight is related also by Saint Ambrose in his Letter XXII to his sister Saint Marcellina, and by Saint Augustine Sermon 286, *City of God,* Book XX, Chapter 8, and *Confessions* Book IX, Chapter 7. Cf. Smith and Wace, *Dictionary of Christian Biography,* IV, 633. s.v. Severus (10). *Note to the 2019 edition:* Augustine suggests that he was an eyewitness to this miracle in Sermon 286: "I was there. I was at Milan. I saw the miracles wrought....A blind man, well known to the whole city, received his sight. He hastened, he got himself guided near. He returned without a guide."

4. The Basilica Ambrosiana was a church within the walls of Milan. The present cathedral of Milan stands upon the site of the primitive episcopal church which Saint Ambrose, in writing to his sister Saint Marcellina, calls the "Grand Basilica." The Church of Saint Ambrose survived until the middle of the fifth century. In AD 452 it was destroyed by the ferocious Attila, when he ravished the fairest portions of Gaul, as well as Pannonia and Venetia, and with fire and sword penetrated into the southern portions of Italy.

    The cathedral of Milan, which had been rebuilt, was again destroyed by fire in 1075. It was for the third time rebuilt in 1162. Cf. *Catholic Encyclopedia,* I, 388.

5. Luke 11:15.
6. Mark 1:24.
7. John 9:29.
8. Matthew 18:6.
9. This treatise is found in the Benedictine Edition under the title *De Incarnationis Dominicae Sacramento, Opera Omnia Ambrosii,* 815–846. That it is the work which Paulinus refers to we know from the opening words of the treatise, *"Debitum, fratres, cupio soluendum, sed hesternos meos non inuenio creditores,"* which are the exact words that Paulinus quotes in the *Vita* as the opening words of the sermon of Saint Ambrose. This undoubtedly is the strongest proof for the authenticity of the *De Incarnationis Dominicae Sacremento.* Cf. Schanz VIII, iv, 1, 346–347; Bardenhewer, III, 535.

CHAPTER VI
HIS LEGATION TO MAXIMUS THE USURPER, AND THE EPISCOPAL ZEAL AGAINST HIM. HE IS A TERROR TO THE DEMONS.

19. And so after the emperor Gratian[1] had been killed, for the sake of recovering his body he undertook a second embassy to Maximus.[2] He who wishes to learn how firmly he dealt with him will determine when he has read the letter of this embassy sent to Valentinian the younger,[3] for it has seemed to us inconsistent with our promise to insert it, lest the prolixity of the letter when added cause irritation to the reader. And Maximus himself he kept from partaking of Communion, admonishing him to do penance for having shed the blood of his master, and—what is worse—an innocent man, if he wished to receive consideration for himself before God. But when he with a haughty spirit refused to do penance, he not only lost salvation for the future but also for the present, and the imperial power which he had wickedly seized, he laid down through fear in the manner of a woman, thereby confessing that he had been the procurator of the state not the emperor.

20. Now when after the death of Justina, a certain sooth-sayer, Innocent[4] by name though not in deed, during a trial for his misdeeds was being put to torture by the judge, he began to confess something different from what he was being asked, for he cried out that greater torments were being applied to him by that angel who was protecting Ambrose, because in the time of Justina, ascending the top of the roof of the church, he had offered sacrifices in the middle of the night to arouse the hatred of the people against the bishop. But the more insistently and assiduously he practiced his malignant work, the greater grew the love

of the people for the Catholic faith and the bishop of the Lord. He confessed that he had also sent demons to kill him but that the demons had reported that they were not only entirely unable to go near him but even could not go near the doors of the house in which the bishop abode because an insurmountable fire completely protected that building so that even though being far off they were burned, and that he thus had given up his artifices by which he thought that he might do something against the bishop of the Lord. Another person also came even to his bedchamber carrying a sword to kill the bishop, but when he had raised his hand he remained there with drawn sword in his stiffened right hand. Then after he had confessed that he had been sent by Justina, the arm which had become stiff as it was being stretched in wickedness, was cured by the confession.

21. At the same time when a certain Probus, a man of high rank, had sent to the bishop his servant, a secretary who was being seriously troubled by an unclean spirit, the devil left him as he departed from the city, fearing to be brought to the holy man. And so as long as the boy was with the bishop in Milan, no power of the devil appeared in him. But when he left Milan and came near the city, the same spirit which had possessed him before began to torment him. And when the devil was questioned by the exorcists,[5] why he had not appeared in him as long as he had been in Milan, he confessed that he had feared Ambrose and therefore had withdrawn for a time and had awaited in that place where he had withdrawn from the boy until he should return, and when he did return he had sought again the vessel which he had deserted.

NOTES

1. Flavius Gratianus Augustus, Roman emperor from 375–383, was the oldest son of Valentinian I. At the age of nine he was named

Chapter VI

Augustus by his father and in 375, at the age of 16, succeeded his father to the throne. His reign is a noteworthy epoch in Church history. He was the first to refuse the robe and title of Pontifex Maximus and became active in suppressing heathen worship by confiscating the revenues of the priests and vestal virgins, together with the landed property of the temples. He removed the altar of the goddess of Victory from the hall of the senate and reduced the immunities of the pagan priests. These alternations, especially the removal of the altar of Victory, occasioned great commotion among the pagans. Shortly after this the emperor lost his life at the hands of the usurper Maximus. He was then but twenty-four years old.

The relations of Saint Ambrose and Gratian had been always tender and affectionate and it was for the latter that Saint Ambrose wrote his great treatise, *De Fide*. Cf. Smith and Wace, *Dictionary of Christian Biography*, II, 721–727.

2. Maximus Magnus Clemens, a native of Spain, is variously represented to us—as the comrade, general, and butler of the emperor. He was proclaimed emperor by the legions in Britain in 383 and at the head of his army crossed into Gaul and attacked Gratian whom he defeated near Paris and finally had slain near Lyons. Maximus next turned his eyes to the possession of Italy which was ruled by Valentinian II. The latter fled to Constantinople to register the help of Theodosius. Meanwhile, Maximus entered Milan and Rome in triumph and consequently all Italy submitted without a struggle.

Maximus remained emperor until 388, when Theodosius, coming to the aid of Valentinian and avenging the death of his colleague, took Aquileia by storm and there had Maximus decapitated. Cf. Smith, *Dictionary of Greek and Roman Biography and Mythology*, II, 996–997.

3. Valentinian II, son of Valentinian I and brother of Gratian, was emperor, from 375–392. However, he was all these years but merely a nominal ruler, for while Valens and later Theodosius ruled in the East, and Gratian and later Maximus had control of much of the West. Italy was the only portion left to Valentinian. After the death of Justina, his Arian mother, Valentinian abandoned Arianism, became a catechumen and invited Saint Ambrose to come to Gaul to administer baptism to him. He was not spared to receive it however, as he died before Saint Ambrose could reach him. There are different accounts of his death but the most probable is that he was strangled by the order of Arbogast, his general, under whose evil influence he fell after the death of Justina. His body was brought to Milan, where Saint Ambrose delivered his funeral oration, *De Obitu Valentiniani*

Consolatio, speaking among other things, about the efficacy of the baptism of desire. Cf. Smith and Wace, *Dictionary of Christian Biography*, IV, 1074–1075; Smith, *Dictionary of Greek and Roman Biography and Mythology,* III, 1210–1211.

4. Innocentius is not mentioned elsewhere. Cf. Smith and Wace, s. v. Innocentius (31).

5. An exorcist is one whose office it was to cast out devils, and he received the right to use the solemn formulæ of the Church for that purpose. In the Western Church the order of exorcist has never been established.

In 398, the fourth Council of Carthage prescribes the rite of ordination for exorcist, which rite has been retained until the present day. Gradually, as conditions changed in the Church, the office of exorcist ceased altogether and was taken over by the clerics in major orders. In our times only priests are authorized to use the exorcising power. *Cf. Catholic Encyclopedia* V, 711–712. The word *exorcista* is Late. It is cited first in the *Justinianic Code,* 1, 3, 6. See Scott, *The Civil Law*.

CHAPTER VII

HIS FAVOR PREVAILS OVER THEODOSIUS, WHOM ON ACCOUNT OF THE MASSACRE OF THE CITIZENS OF THESSALONICA HE DEPRIVES OF PARTICIPATION OF THE SACRAMENTS. THE FAME OF THE HOLY BISHOP REACHES EVEN TO THE PERSIANS.

22. Now when Maximus had been executed and the emperor Theodosius was at Milan and Bishop Ambrose was at Aquileia,[1] in the regions of the East in a certain fortified city, the Jewish synagogue and a grove of the Valentinians[2] were burned by the Christians because either the Jews or the Valentinians had insulted the Christian monks, for the Valentinian heretics worship thirty gods. And the Count of the East sent a report of the act to the emperor who, when he received it, ordered the synagogue to be rebuilt by the bishop of the place and moreover, that punishment be exacted of the monks. But when the tenor of this order had

Chapter VII

reached the ears of the venerable man, Bishop Ambrose, he dispatched a letter to the emperor[3] because he himself was unable to hasten forth at that time, in which he requested of him that what had been decreed by him should be recalled, and stated that an audience should be reserved for himself by him who, if he were unworthy to be heard by him, would also be unworthy to be heard in his behalf by the Lord or to whomever he should entrust his entreaties and prayers. Furthermore, that he was prepared to undergo death for such a matter, lest by his negligence he might make an apostate out of the emperor who had given such unjust orders against the Church.

23. However, after he had returned to Milan and when the emperor was present in the church, he preached in the presence of the people on this same subject. In this discourse he introduced the person of our Lord as speaking to the emperor: "I made you emperor from the lowest, I delivered the army of your enemy to you, I gave to you the troops which he had prepared as his army against you, I brought your enemy into your power, I placed one of your seed on the throne of the empire, I made you triumph without labor, and do you give triumphs to my enemies over me?"

The emperor said to him as he descended from the pulpit:[4] "You spoke against us today, bishop."

But he answered that he had not spoken against him but for him.

Then the emperor said: "Truly, I gave a stern command to the bishop on the restoration of the synagogue, moreover that the punishment must be exacted of the monks." So too it was reported by the counts who were present at the time.

The bishop said to them: "I now treat, of course, with the emperor, but with you I must treat otherwise." And so he contrived that the orders which had been given should be recalled, and he said that he would not approach the altar unless the emperor should show by his promise that he ought to go on. And the bishop said to him: "Shall I therefore go on, with your promise?"

The emperor answered: "Go on, with my promise." After this solemn promise had been repeated the bishop now, without anxiety, performed the divine mysteries. These things, however, were written in a letter which he sent to his sister,[5] and it he enclosed the sermon which he had preached on that same day about the staff of the nut tree which is described as having been seen by the prophet Jeremias.[6]

24. At the same time on account of the city of Thessalonica, no little distress came upon the bishop when he learned that the city had been almost wiped out. For the emperor had promised him that he would grant pardon to the citizens of the above mentioned city, but when the counts had consulted secretly with the emperor without the knowledge of the bishop the city was given to the sword for almost three hours and many innocent were slain. When the bishop learned of this deed he refused the emperor any opportunity of entering the church, nor did he judge him worthy of union with the church or of the participation in the sacraments before he should do public penance. On the other hand, the emperor declared to him that David had committed adultery and also homicide. But straightway the reply was given: "You who have followed him as he sinned, follow him as he corrected himself." When the most merciful emperor heard this he so took it to heart that he did not scorn public penance, and the progress of this correction prepared for him a favorable victory.[7]

25. At the same time two of the most powerful and wisest men of the Persians, because of the fame of the bishop, came to Milan bringing with them many questions that thereby they might make a trial of wisdom of the great

Chapter VII

man, and with him they argued through an interpreter from the first hour of the day until the third hour of the night, and they went away full of wonder. And to show that they had come for no other reason than really to get better acquainted with the man of whom they had heard by report, on the next day bidding farewell to the emperor they set out for the city of Rome, wishing there to become acquainted with the power of the illustrious man Probus. And when they had become acquainted with it they returned to their own home.

NOTES

1. Aquileia, situated at the head of the Adriatic, was founded by the Romans in 182 BC as a bulwark against the northern barbarians. It was made one of the strongest fortresses of the Romans and, due to its position, it became a most flourishing commercial center. Aquileia for many centuries was the seat of a famous Western patriarchate, for which reason it plays an important role in ecclesiastical history.

   Tradition tells us that Saint Mark, sent thither by Saint Peter, founded this see of which Saint Hermagoras is considered the first bishop. In the fourth century this city was the chief ecclesiastical center for the region about the head of the Adriatic. In AD 381 it was the seat of a famous council held against the Arians attended by thirty-two or (twenty-four) bishops.

   Aquileia was taken and completely destroyed by Attila in 452, its inhabitants escaping to the lagoons, where Venice was later built. Cf. *Catholic Encyclopedia,* I, 661–662.
2. Valentinians, the best known and most influential Gnostic heretics, had their own origin with Valentinus. Probably born in Egypt and trained in Hellenistic science in Alexandria, he remained in Rome for about fifteen years trying to establish his heretical system, as a result of which he was excommunicated. He resumed his activities in Cyprus and died there about AD 160 or 161.

   Valentinus believed and taught that the Primal Being, or Bythos, after ages of silence and contemplation, gave rise to other beings by process of emanation. The æons, or the first series of beings, were thirty in number, representing fifteen syzygies, or pairs, sexually complementary. Through the sin of Sophia, one of the lowest aeons, the lower world was brought into existence. Man was considered the highest being in the lower world and the work of redemption was to free the higher, or spiritual, from the servitude of the lower, which redemption was to be brought about by Christ and the Holy Ghost. Valentinus had many disciples even during his lifetime and his heresy spread through Egypt, Syria, Asia Minor, Italy, and Southern Gaul. *Cf. Catholic Encyclopedia*, XV, 256.

3. Cf. Letter XL of Saint Ambrose to Theodosius in which he discusses the decision respecting the restoration of the Jewish synagogue. He also touches on the temple of the Valentinians, whom he declares to be worse than the heathens.

Note to the 2019 edition: It should be recalled that at this time, Christians and Jews were at dagger's points, considering each other to be mortal enemies. In the mid-4th century, each side had attempted to influence Roman imperial policy to the detriment of the other. In the letter cited above, Ambrose alludes to an incident during the reign of Julian the Apostate who, to the delight of the Jews, sought to rebuild the Temple in Jerusalem in an attempt to falsify Christian prophecy. This attempt was foiled by an earthquake and fire which demolished the works. See the *Ecclesiastical History* of Sozomen, Book V, Chapter 22. As a matter of policy, Julian also demanded that Christians at their own expense rebuild pagan temples that had been destroyed (see Sozomen, Book V, Chapter 5). Thus, it is likely that Ambrose's forceful reaction to Theodosius's command that the Christian community of Callinicum rebuild the synagogue and the temple of the Valentinians had its genesis in the similar policies of Julian a mere 20 years before.

4. The term used in the original manuscript is *exedra*. An *exedra* originally was an alcove in a Greek gymnasium where philosophers sat to talk with their disciples. Later, a conversation hall furnished with seats was called an *exedra*. We also read of a place leading out of a portico where philosophers and rhetoricians debated or addressed the people as being termed *exedra*. Cicero had a little *exedra* built in his house at Tusculum and from him we learn that people liked to furnish the *exedra* with couches, where they were accustomed to take their afternoon siesta. How it came to be used in connection with the Christian Church is uncertain. It is probable, though we have no evidence of this, that among the Christians it was a custom to call *exedra* that part of the basilica which was separated from the main hall of the edifice and which later gave birth to the apse of the basilica, and finally from this developed the choir furnished with stalls for the clergy or the dignitaries.

Exedra was also a name given to a little isolated semi-circular construction more or less decorated, sometimes sheltered, found here and there in cities. Perhaps it is then from the latter that the *exedra*

CHAPTER VII

took its form and name, since in the early Christian basilicas a semi-circular construction covered by a canopy, beautifully decorated, was called an *exedra.* Cf. Cabrol, *Dictionnaire d'Archéologie Chrétienne et De Liturgie,* V, 951; *Catholic Encyclopedia,* V, 692.

5. Cf. Letter XLI of Ambrose to his sister Marcellina in which he himself relates the circumstances and the scene, telling her also of his sermon before the Emperor and his refusal to celebrate Holy Mass until the Emperor had promised to recall the order. *Ergo ago fide tua? Age fide mea,* are the very expressions found in this letter and which Paulinus quotes in the Vita—that is, "Shall I therefore go on, with your promise?" "Go on, with my promise."

6. Jeremiah 1:11.

7. The details of the penance of Theodosius have been variously presented to us by the early historians, Theodoret, Rufinus, and Sozomen. It is difficult to determine the source of these details but some modern critics are inclined to believe that the statement of Paulinus: "he refused the emperor any opportunity for entering the church" (*copiam imperator ingrediendi ecclesiam denegauit*), is responsible for the existing legend that Saint Ambrose forbade Theodosius to set foot within the church, "who in all probability," as De Labriolle (*Saint Ambroise,* 145) writes, "did no more than freely paraphrase Letter 51 of Saint Ambrose." The whole question of the Penance of Theodosius is discussed by Mannix, Sr. M. Dolorosa, *Sancti Ambrosii Oratio de Obitu Theodosii,* 9–21, where this passage of Paulinus also receives due consideration. In the latter we find a brief synopsis of the incident, the account of the early historians and the testimony of Saint Ambrose himself.

Note to the 2019 edition: A modern English translation of Ambrose's Funeral Oration for Theodosius the Great may be found as part of McCauley et al.: *Funeral Orations by Saint Gregory Nazianzen and Saint Ambrose,* 1968.

CHAPTER VIII

HE FIRMLY RESISTS SYMMACHUS, THE PREFECT OF THE CITY, WHO URGES THE RESTITUTION OF THE ALTAR OF VICTORY. HE FINDS THE RELICS OF THE HOLY MARTYRS. THROUGH HIS FAVOR WITH GOD AND HIS AUTHORITY, HE PREVAILS OVER THE EMPEROR AND THE QUEEN OF THE MARCOMANNI.

26. But when Theodosius had left Italy and was at Constantinople, an embassy was sent to the emperor Valentinian who was in Gaul, in the name of the Senate by Symmachus,[1] then the Prefect of the city,[2] regarding the restitution of the altar of Victory[3] and the maintenance of the sacred rites. But when the bishop found this out, he sent a petition to the emperor and demanded that copies of the report be sent to him, to which he himself for his part would reply. When he received this report he wrote a most splendid letter[4] so that Symmachus, eloquent as he was, dared answer nothing in reply. But after Valentinian of sacred memory had ended his life in the city of Vienna, which is a city of the Gauls, Eugenius[5] ascended the throne. He, not long after he begun to reign, when Flavian[6] the Prefect of that time and Count Arbogast[7] made petition for the altar of Victory and the maintenance of the sacred rites—a thing which Valentinian of sacred memory, while still tender in years, had denied them when they petitioned him—forgetful of his faith, granted their request.

27. When the bishop learned this, leaving the city of Milan to which Eugenius had come in haste, he set out for the city of Bononia[8] and thence proceeded as far as Faventia.[9] And when he spent a few days there, at the invitation of the Florentines, he went down to Tuscia,[10]

Chapter VIII

avoiding rather the sight of the sacrilegious man and not fearing injury from the emperor. For he even sent him a letter[11] in which he addressed his conscience, from which I think that a few of the many points should be quoted here. "Even if the imperial power is great, yet consider, Emperor, how great is God. He sees the hearts of all, He examines their interior conscience, He knows all things before they happen, He knows the secrets of your heart. You do not allow yourself to be deceived and you wish to conceal things from God? Has nothing come to your mind? If they acted so persistently, was it not your duty, Emperor, to oppose more persistently for the worship of God, the most high and the true and the living, and to refuse what was to the injury of the Holy Law?" And again: "Since then I am bound by my words both before God and before men, I thought nothing else was permitted to me, nothing else proper, but to look to my own welfare since I could not look to yours."

28. And in the above mentioned city of Florence, while he stayed in the home of the late Decens who was a man of high rank and what is more, a Christian, his son, Pansophius by name still a mere child when he was laboring with an unclean spirit, was cured by repeated prayers and by the bishop himself imposing his hands.[12] But some days after, seized by sudden illness, the little child breathed forth his soul. And his mother, who was very pious and full of faith and the fear of God, taking him descended from the upper to the lower part of the house and placed him on the bed of the bishop in his absence. When on his return the bishop found him there on his bed—for he had been out of the house at that time—full of pity for the mother and witnessing her faith, like Elisæus, he laid himself down on the body of the child and through prayer succeeded in returning alive to the mother the child, whom he had found was dead. And for this child also he wrote a little book so that what he was

not able to realize on account of his infant age, he might learn through reading. Nevertheless, he did not mention the occurrence in his writings, but on what consideration he refused to mention it, it is not ours to judge.

29. In the same city also he founded a basilica in which he placed the relics of the martyrs Vitalis and Agricola,[13] whose bodies he had raised in the city of Bologna. For the bodies of the martyrs had been buried among the bodies of the Jews, nor would it have been known to the Christian people, if the holy martyrs had not revealed themselves to the bishop of that church. When they were placed under the altar which had been built in this same basilica, great delight and rejoicing was there on the part of all the faithful and punishment of the demons confessing the merits of the martyrs.

30. At the same time Count Arbogast prepared war against his people, namely the Franks, and he valiantly routed no small number in battle and with the rest he made peace. But when at a banquet he was asked by the princes of his nation whether he knew Ambrose, and he replied that he knew the man and was loved by him and was wont to dine with him frequently, he heard: "So you conquer, Count, because you are beloved by that man who says to the sun: 'stand' and it stands."[14] And so I have set this down that my readers may know what fame the holy man had even among barbarian peoples. For we also know this on the report of a certain young man of Arbogast, very religious, who was present, for at the time at which they said these things he was a cupbearer.

31. And so the bishop having set out from Tuscia returned to Milan, because Eugenius had already departed thence against Theodosius. There he awaited the coming of the Christian emperor, secure through the power of God, because He does not give up those who believe in Him to

Chapter VIII

the unjust, nor *does He let fall the rod of sinners on the lot of the just, that the just may not stretch forth their hands to iniquity.*[15] For Arbogast, Count at that time, and the Prefect Flavian had promised as they were leaving Milan, that when they should return victorious, they would make a stable in the basilica of the church of Milan and would review the clergy under arms. But when the wretched men become wickedly credulous of their demons and *open their mouths in blasphemy against God,*[16] they deprive themselves of hope of victory. Moreover the cause for their disturbance was this: because the gifts of the emperor,[17] who had involved himself in the sacrilege,[18] were spurned by the Church nor was association with the Church in prayer granted him. But the Lord who is wont to protect His Church *cast His judgment from heaven*[19] and transferred complete victory to the pious emperor Theodosius. And so after Eugenius and his satellites were crushed, when he received letters from the emperor, he had no greater care than to intercede for those whom he found under impeachment. However, sending a deacon, he first besought the emperor by letter.[20] But after John,[21] at that time a tribune and secretary but who is now a Prefect, had been sent to protect those who took refuge in the church, he himself went to Aquileia to intercede for them. And pardon was easily obtained for them, because the Christian emperor casting himself at the feet of the bishop bore witness that he had been saved by his merits and prayers.

32. And so returning from the city of Aquileia, he arrived one day before the emperor. And the emperor Theodosius of most kind memory, after his sons were received into the Church and entrusted to the bishop, was not long in this life. And after his death Ambrose survived about three years. At this time he raised and transferred the body of Saint Nazarius,[22] the martyr, which had been buried

in a garden outside the city to the Basilica of the Apostles which is near the Roman Gate. We saw, moreover, in the grave in which the body of the martyr lay—although when he suffered, we cannot learn even to this day—the blood of the martyr as fresh as if it had been shed on that very day. His head also, which had been severed by the wicked, was so whole and uncorrupted with hair and beard that it seemed to us that it had been washed and placed in the grave at the very moment at which it was dug up. And why should this be strange, since the Lord indeed has already promised this in the Gospel, that *a hair from their heads shall not perish?*[23] We were also suffused with such a wondrous odor that it surpassed the sweetness of all perfumes.

33. When this body of the martyr was dug up and laid on a litter, we immediately proceeded with the holy bishop to the martyr Saint Celsus,[24] who was buried in the same garden, to pray. We have learned, however, that never before had he prayed in that very place, and this was the sign of the discovery of a martyr, namely, if the holy bishop should go to pray to a place at which he had never been before. We know, however, from the custodians of the place, that it was a tradition with them from their parents, not to depart from that place from generation to generation of their people on this account because great treasures had been buried there. And indeed great treasures they were, which neither rust nor the worm destroys nor thieves dig up and steal, because Christ is their guardian and their habitation is the court of heaven, *for whom it was Christ to live and to die was gain.*[25] And so after the body of the martyr was transported to the Basilica of the Apostles,[26] where previously the relics of the Holy Apostles had been deposited with the greatest devotion of all, while the bishop was preaching one of the populace filled with an unclean spirit began to cry out that he was tormented by Ambrose. But he turned to him and

CHAPTER VIII

said: "Be silent, devil, because Ambrose does not torment thee, but the faith of the saints and thy envy, because you see men rise to that place whence you have been cast down, for Ambrose knows not how to be puffed up." After these words, he who was crying out became silent and threw himself upon the ground and no longer uttered a sound by which he might cause disturbance.

34. At the same time, when the emperor Honorius[27] in the time of his consulship was giving an exhibition of wild beasts from Libya in the city of Milan, as the people assembled there, permission was then given to the soldiers who had been sent for the purpose by Count Stilicho[28] at the request of Eusebius[29] the Prefect, to take a certain Cresconius[30] from the church. And as he took refuge at the altar of the Lord, the holy bishop with the clergy who were present at the time surrounded him for defense. But the multitude of soldiers, who had members of the Arian heresy as their leaders, prevailed against the few and carrying Cresconius away in exultation returned to the amphitheater, leaving no small sorrow to the Church, for the bishop prostrate before the altar of the Lord long bemoaned the deed. But when the soldiers had returned and reported to those by whom they had been sent, the leopards on being set loose leaped with a swift bound to the very place in which they who were triumphing over the Church had taken their seats and left them severely lacerated. Then when Count Stilicho saw this he was moved with repentance so that for many days he made apologies to the bishop and even dismissed unharmed him who had been carried off. But because he was guilty of the most heinous crimes and could not be chastised otherwise, he sent him into exile, although pardon followed not long after.

35. At the same time, as he was going to the palace and we were following him by virtue of our office, when

a certain man slipped by chance and lay prostrate on the ground, the bishop turned to Theodulus[31]—at that time a notary, although afterwards he ruled the church of Mutina[32] with the greatest esteem—who was laughing at the mishap, and said: "And you who stand, see that you do not fall." When he said this, immediately he who laughed at the fall of another grieved at his own.

36. At the same time, Frigitil,[33] a certain queen of the Marcomanni,[34] when she heard of the fame of the man from the report of a certain Christian who had by chance come to her from the regions of Italy, believed in Christ whose servant she recognized him to be, and sending gifts to the Church she asked through her envoys that she be informed by his own hand what she should believe. And to her he wrote a remarkable letter in the manner of a catechism, in which he urged her also to persuade her husband to keep peace with the Romans. When the woman received the letter she persuaded her husband to entrust himself and his people to the Romans. When she came to Milan, she grieved very much because she did not find the holy bishop to whom she had hastened, for he had already departed from his life.

37. Now in the time of Gratian, to retrace my steps, when he had come to the residence of Macedonius,[35] at that time the Master of the Offices,[36] to intercede for a certain man and had found the doors closed by the order of the official mentioned above and obtained no opportunity to enter, he said: "You also indeed will come to the Church, and since the doors have been closed, you will not find whereby you may enter." And this came to pass, for at the death of Gratian, Macedonius on fleeing to a church could not find the entrance although the doors were open.

NOTES

1. Aurelius Q. Symmachus, who flourished in the latter half of the

Chapter VIII

fourth century AD, was a distinguished scholar, statesman, and orator. He held the office of quæstor, prætor, corrector of Lucania and Bruttii, pro-consul of Africa, and in 383 or 384 was Prefect of the City. In 391 Theodosius raised him to the consulship. In all these offices he bore himself modestly, performed his duties with mildness, firmness, and integrity, seldom found among statesman of his age. He was chosen by the Senate to remonstrate with Gratian and with Valentinian on the removal of the altar of Victory from the Senate but was unsuccessful and his zeal for the pagan religion involved him in no little danger and disgrace.

From the writings of Symmachus there are extant ten books of epistles which give us a remarkable picture of the circumstances and life of a Roman noble before the break-up of the empire. We also have three panegyrics on Valentinian I, and Gratian, and a number of *relationes* or official reports of Symmachus as *præfectus urbi* to the Emperor. Cf. Smith and Wace, *Dictionary of Christian Biography*, IV, 749–751.

We read in the *Confessions* (Book V, Chapter 13) of Saint Augustine that when the people of Milan sent a petition for a state-appointed teacher of rhetoric, Symmachus, then Prefect of Rome, sent Augustine.

2. The office of the Prefect of the city is one of the oldest in Rome. In the monarchial period the Prefect was the substitute of the king, while in the Republic, the two consuls when leaving the city delegated one to represent them in their absence. The Prefect was then vested with all the powers of the consuls. Under the Empire likewise, the Emperor appointed a Prefect to maintain order during his absence from the city, and finally we read that Tiberius made the *præfectus urbi* a permanent official. The chief function of this official was to maintain order in the city of Rome, hence his duties required taking charge of public gatherings at the markets, theaters and circus. Naturally, his functions concerned with police control, later acquired criminal jurisdiction, which did not, however, supplant the jurisdiction of the ordinary courts. Cf. Greenidge, *The Student's Gibbon*, I, 169–170; Abbot's *Political Institutions*, 18, 246, 339, 349, 449.

3. The Altar of Victory had its origin after the battle of Actium 29 BC, when Augustus erected in the Senate house an altar, above which stood a statue representing Victory.

In AD 382 Gratian ordered the removal of the famous altar of Victory and also forbade the people to contribute to the maintenance of heathen sacrifices and withdrew from the priests and vestal virgins their revenues. These measures aroused the indignation of the pagans. They sent a deputation headed by Symmachus to remonstrate against the edicts. The party was not received by Gratian.

In 384 the pagan party in the Senate again began to hope for a repeal of the hostile measure of Gratian, and presented their plea for toleration and the restoration of the altar of Victory to Valentinian II. Again the petition availed nothing, as Saint Ambrose, hearing of this, addressed a letter to the Emperor (Epist. XVII) warning him against the restoration. And in a second letter (Epist. XVIII) he gives a complete answer to the arguments of Symmachus.

In 393 Eugenius restored the altar but did not recover the confiscated revenues. The altar was finally removed by Theodosius after the downfall of Eugenius. Cf. De Labriolle, *Saint Ambroise*, 35–71; Hodgkin, *Italy and Her Invaders*, Book I, Volume 1. 397, 416, 560.

4. Cf. Letter XVII to Valentinian II in which Saint Ambrose reminds the Emperor that it is his business to defend religion, not superstition. He warns Valentinian that if he answers to the petition of the pagans he will incur the censures of the Church, and will be acting in a manner derogatory to the memory of his father and brother.

5. Formerly a rhetorician, Eugenius was constituted the chief secretary to the Emperor. He associated with himself Arbogast, who then had command of a division of the army, and determined to usurp the government. These two then brought about the murder of Valentinian II and Eugenius immediately assumed the supreme authority in the western parts of the empire. Hearing this, Theodosius hurried to Italy and in this war Eugenius was defeated, taken prisoner, and put to death in 394. He held the power for two years. Cf. Smith, *Dictionary of Greek and Roman Biography and Mythology*, II, 169; *Cambridge Mediaeval History*, Vol. 1, *Christian Era*, 246–247.

6. Flavianus, Prætorian Prefect of Italy and Illyricum in 382–383, was a zealous pagan and strong supporter of the usurper Eugenius. He persuaded the latter to take up arms against Theodosius, assuring him of his success. It is believed by historians that Flavian perished by his own hand in the war of Eugenius against Theodosius in 394. Cf. Smith, *Dictionary of Greek and Roman Biography and Mythology*, s. v. Flavianus (31); Smith and Wace, *Dictionary of Christian Biography*, II, 535.

7. Arbogast, a Frankish general, was put in command of the troops in Gaul by Theodosius. He possessed many good qualities: he was a man of reckless courage, a master of the art of war, but he was after all a hard, rough barbarian and intensely fond of power. So having

Chapter VIII

removed all those who were faithful to Valentinian II, then Emperor, Arbogast caused him to be murdered and acknowledged Eugenius as Emperor. Theodosius, after two years preparation, marched into Italy and in 394 defeated the usurper's troops. Eugenius was beheaded and Arbogast killed himself. Cf. Bury's *Cambridge Mediaeval History, Vol. I Christian Era,* 243–246. Hodgkin, *Italy and Her Invaders*, Book I, Volume 1, 550–554.

8. Bononia, modern Bologna, is the principal city of the province of the same name. The history of the beginnings of Christianity in Bologna are uncertain. Saint Zama is said to have been the first bishop of Bologna, who according to some was ordained about 207. It is certain, however, that the episcopate dates back to an earlier date than 207. The episcopal see of Bologna was first subject to Milan but later it recognized the authority of the Metropolitan of Ravenna. Cf. *Catholic Encyclopedia,* II, 639–641.

9. Faventia, or modern Faenza, is in the province of Ravenna. As early as 82 BC Faenza is mentioned in the report of the victory of Sulla over the consul Cneius Papirius Carbo. The early history of the development of Christianity is obscure. The first historically certain bishop is Constantius, who was present at a council in Rome 313, and Saint Savinus is considered his predecessor. We also read of another Constantius, bishop of Faenza, who was a contemporary of Saint Ambrose. Cf. *Catholic Encyclopedia* V, 751.

10. Tuscia or ancient Etruria under the Empire formed the seventh region of Italy. Ecclesiastically, Tuscia is divided into the provinces of Florence, Pisa, Siena, archdiocese of Lucca, dioceses of Arezzo, Cortona, Montalcino, Montepulciano and Pienza. cf. *Catholic Encyclopedia,* XV, 103–105.

11. Cf. Letter LVII of Saint Ambrose in which he informs the Emperor Eugenius why he absented himself from Milan. Next he reproves the Emperor for his conduct with regard to heathen worship, and then promises to treat him in the future with the same freedom as the other emperors.

12. Imposition of hands is an extremely ancient custom, having come down from patriarchal times. Our Lord Himself healed at first by laying on of hands. The rite has had a secular as well as sacred usage. This custom has a very broad application, being employed by the Church not only where the sacramental rite demands it but almost in all the various blessings of persons and things. Those possessed with an evil spirit are similarly exorcised. Cf. *Catholic Encyclopedia,* VII, 698; Cabrol, *Dict. d' Archéologie Chrétienne et de Liturgie,* VII, 391–413.

13. Saints Vitalis and Agricola were martyred during Diocletian's reign

about 304. Vitalis was a slave of Agricola, a Christian, who because of the gentleness of his master became greatly attached to him and finally embraced the Christian faith. Vitalis was first executed in the amphitheater, and after trying in vain to win over Agricola, the persecutors finally crucified him. Both martyrs were buried in a Jewish graveyard and remained there until 393. Saint Ambrose and bishop Eusebius of Bologna transferred the bodies of the martyrs to a church. Saint Ambrose took a portion of the cross and the nails and some blood to Florence and placed them in the church erected by the widow Juliana. The feast of the martyrs is observed on November 4. Saint Ambrose mentions the two martyrs in his oration, *Exhortatio Virginitatis*, which seems to be the only source for the lives of these two martyrs. Cf. *Catholic Encyclopedia,* XV, 486; Smith and Wace, *Dictionary of Christian Biography,* IV, 1163.
14. Joshua 10:12–13.
15. Psalms 124:3.
16. Apocalypse 13:6.
17. i.e., Eugenius.
18. Eugenius had consented to the restoration of the Altar of Victory.
19. Psalms 75:9.
20. Cf. Letter LXI to Theodosius in which Ambrose explains the reason for his absence from Milan, and having expressed his thankfulness for the success in the war with Eugenius, he urges the Emperor Theodosius to be merciful to the conquered.
21. In 394 John was the tribune and notary to Emperor Theodosius. In 408 we read that he was sent by the Roman Senate as a messenger to Alaric and in 409 the usurper Attalus nominated him Master of Offices. Honorius raised him to the office of Prætorian Prefect, which duty he held from June 6, 412 to June 12, 413. (*Theodosian Code*, XIII, 11, 13; III, 8, 3; XVI, 8, 20.) On July 11, 442, he was again nominated to this office of Praetorian Prefect. Cf. Pauly-Wissowa, IX, 1744 s.v. (4).
22. The only historical information which we possess regarding Saints Nazarius and Celsus, who is mentioned in the subsequent paragraph, is the discovery of their bodies by Saint Ambrose. No doubt there was a tradition regarding these martyrs among Christians of Milan, which led to the finding of the two bodies. A later legend, however, places the martyrdom of these Saints during the persecution of Nero, but this has no historical foundation. It was believed that both Saints were beheaded in Milan and their bodies were buried separately in a garden without the wall, where Saint Ambrose discovered and raised them up in 395. The bodies of the two martyrs were conveyed by Saint Ambrose into the new church of the Apostles, which he

had just built. Cf. *Catholic Encyclopedia,* X, 728; Smith and Wace, *Dictionary of Christian Biography,* IV, 8.
23. Luke 22:18. Luke 12:7. Matthew 10:30.
24. Saint Celsus is treated in connection with Saint Nazarius. Cf. note 22 above.
25. Philippians 1:21.
26. The Church of the Apostles was built by Saint Ambrose in 382 on the model of the church of the Apostles at Constantinople. Later it was dedicated to Saint Nazarius and in the eleventh century it was entirely rebuilt, though it retains with modification the cross form. Cf. Lowrie, *Monuments of the Early Church,* 148.
27. Flavius Honorius was the younger son of Theodosius the Great. The latter divided the empire in 395, allotting the western half to Honorius and the eastern to Arcadius. Honorius died in 424.
28. Stilicho, son of a Vandal, entered the service of the Emperor Valens and distinguished himself in many campaigns against the Visigoths. Because of his great abilities as general and civil administrator he became dear to the army and invaluable to the Emperor Theodosius. It is stated that Theodosius on his death-bed gave to Stilicho a general charge to watch over the safety of the East and West, constituting him in a certain degree guardian of Arcadius and Honorius. In 400 he was raised to the consulship and again in 405 he was elected to the same office. With the death of Arcadius the greatness of Stilicho begins to decline. Being accused of treason he was kept in honorable confinement until finally he was sentenced by Honorius as deserving of death, and shortly after was beheaded. Cf. Smith, *Dictionary of Greek and Roman Biography and Mythology,* III, 911–913; Hodgkin, *Italy and Her Invaders,* Book I, Volume 2, 673–675, 757–760.
29. Eusebius was an official of some rank at the court of Honorius in 395 (*Theodosian Code,* XV, 1, 32) and in the years 395–396 he was the Praetorian Prefect of Italy. Cf. Pauly-Wissowa VI, 1369 s.v. (15), where the present passage is also cited.
30. Cresconius, it seems, is only mentioned here.
31. Theodulus was the secretary of Saint Ambrose for a time and later became the bishop of Mutina, where he was held in high esteem by all. Cf. Tillemont, X, 88, 257, 279.
32. Mutina is the modern city of Modena. It is a diocese in the province of Aemilia.
33. Paulinus is our only source of information for Queen Fritigil of the Macromanni. Cf. Pauly-Wissowa, s.v.
34. Marcomanni (Men of the Marches) was a tribe of the Suebi, whose name first appears in Cæsar's enumeration of the people led by

Ariovistus. Their country, the Marca, extended south to the Danube. Cf. *Cambridge Mediaeval History I, The Christian Roman Empire,* 196.

35. According to Sulpicius Severus (*Sacred History,* Book II, Chapter 48 and 49), Macedonius was the Master of Offices for a longer time before Emperor Maximus came to the throne. Later he seems to have become very bitter and unjust to the Christians, favoring the heretics in every way possible. After the death of Gratian he sought refuge in the church but not being able to find the entrance was seized and brought before Symmachus, the Prefect of the city at the time. Most probably, he was condemned to death as nothing more is heard about him after this. Cf. Rauschen, *Jahrbücher der Christlichen Kirche* (1897), 125, 141, 150–151.

36. The duty of the Master of Offices was the administration of public affairs. He was the chief magistrate of the palace. It was his duty to look after or inspect the discipline of the civil and military schools. All the appeals from those privileged persons who had obtained the right to decline the authority of the ordinary judges were addressed to him from all the parts of the empire. The correspondence between the ruler and his subjects was likewise looked after by him. Cf. Greenidge, *Student's Gibbon* I, 164; Boak, *Two Studies in Later Roman and Byzantine Administration,* 1–160.

CHAPTER IX

THE VIRTUES OF THE HOLY BISHOP. HIS ABSTINENCE, HIS ZEAL IN DIVINE AFFAIRS, HIS CONTEMPT FOR RICHES, HIS MERCY TOWARD OTHERS. HE IS RESPLENDENT WITH THE GRACE OF HIS BLESSINGS.

38. Moreover the venerable bishop himself was a man of great abstinence and many vigils and labors, wearing out his body by daily fasts, whose habit was never to take breakfast except on the day of Sabbath and the Lord's Day, or when the birthdays of the most celebrated martyrs occurred. His constancy in prayer also was great, day and night. He did not shun the work of writing books with his own hand, unless when his body was hindered by some infirmity.[1] There was also in him a solicitude for all the churches, also great and

Chapter IX

unceasing constancy in intervening among them. He was most steadfast also in fulfilling his religious duties, to such a degree that what he alone had been accustomed to perform as regards to those he baptized, five bishops after the time of his death performed with difficulty. He was exceedingly solicitous too for the poor and the captives, for at the time when he was consecrated bishop, all the gold and silver which he could have kept he gave to the church or to the poor. The estates also which he had, having reserved their usufruct for his sister, he gave to the church, leaving nothing for himself which he could call his own in this world, that like a lightly clad and unencumbered soldier he might follow Christ the Lord: *Who, being rich, became poor for our sakes, that through His poverty we might be rich.*[2]

39. *He rejoiced also with those that rejoiced and wept with those that wept,*[3] since indeed, as often as anyone confessed his sins to him to receive a penance, he so wept that he compelled that one to weep—he seemed to himself to be prostrate with the prostrate. Cases of crime, however, which anyone confessed to him, he told to no one except to the Lord alone with whom he pleaded, leaving a good example to future bishops that they should be intercessors before God rather than accusers before men.[4] For according to the Apostle also, *charity is to be confirmed toward a man of this kind,*[5] because he himself is his own accuser and does not wait for an accuser but anticipates him, that he himself may lighten his sin by confession lest he have something which his adversary may charge against him. And therefore, Scripture says: *"The just is first accuser of his own word."*[6] For he takes away the words of his adversary and he crushes as it were, by the confession of his sins, the teeth prepared for the prey of accursed calumny, giving honor to God to whom all things are open and who wishes the life rather than the death of the sinner. For confession alone is not

sufficient for him who repents, unless a correction in deed follows, so that on repenting he may not perform deeds that must needs be repented, and may also humble his soul like holy David, who after he heard from the prophet: *"Your sin is pardoned,"*[7] in the correction of his sin became more humble so that *he did eat ashes like bread and mingled his drink with weeping.*[8]

40. He also wept most bitterly as often as by chance announcement was made to him of the death of any holy bishop—so much so that we would strive to console him, ignorant of the pious affection of the man and not knowing for what reason he so wept. And to us he would give a reply of this nature: that he did not weep because the one who had been announced as dead had departed, but he had gone before him and because it was difficult to find a man who might be regarded as worthy of the high dignity of the episcopacy. He himself, moreover, spoke beforehand of his death, saying that he would be with us until Easter—and this indeed merited through his prayer to the Lord, that he might be freed earlier from this life.

41. For he lamented vehemently whenever he saw that avarice was flourishing, the root of all evil, which can be diminished neither by abundance nor want, and was increasing more and more among men especially among those who had been placed in authority, so that it was a most difficult task for him to prevent it among these because all things were being torn asunder for gain. And this thing first brought all evil to Italy, and from it all things are inclined toward the worse. And what shall I say, if it works its madness thus in persons of this kind who are wont to offer as pretexts children or relatives: *To make excuses in sins,*[9] since indeed it has seized even many celibates, bishops, and deacons whose portion is God, so that they themselves practice it. And woe to us in our wretchedness! Because not

Chapter IX

even at the end of the world are we summoned, although we wish to be freed from so heavy a yoke of slavery which sinks even into the *depths of hell,*[10] that *we may make for ourselves friends of the mammon of iniquity, that they may receive us into everlasting dwellings.*[11] And yet *blessed is he who* when on being converted, having broken the chains and having flung down the yoke of such domination, *shall take and dash his little ones against the rock,*[12] that is, shall dash all his thoughts against *Christ*, who according to the Apostle is the rock which destroys all dashed against it, itself remaining unharmed and not making him guilty who had dashed against it the meaner offspring of his worthless womb but innocent, so that he may confidently say: *"The Lord is my portion,"*[13] because to whom there is nothing in the world, to him truly Christ is the portion, and he who shall despise few things will receive many and besides *shall even possess life eternal.*[14]

42. But a few days before he was confined to his bed, while he was dictating the 43rd Psalm and I was taking it down and observing him, suddenly a fire in the shape of a small shield covered his head and gradually it entered through his mouth like a householder into his home, after which his face became like snow, but afterwards his countenance returned to its normal appearance. When this happened, being struck with amazement I became stiff and was unable to write down what was being spoken by him until after the vision itself has passed, for he at that time was giving the testimony of the divine Scriptures which I remembered very well. For he put an end to writing and dictating on that day, since he could not finish that psalm. I, however, immediately related that which had been seen by me to the honorable man Castus the deacon,[15] under whose care I lived and he, filled with the grace of God, explained from his reading of the Acts of the Apostles that I had seen

in the bishop the coming of the Holy Spirit.

43. Sometime before, moreover, when a servant of the then Count Stilicho, who had been troubled with a demon, was abiding already cured in the Ambrosian Basilica at the recommendation of his master, he was reported indeed—and this was freely believed by his master—to be forging letters of the tribunate, so that men who were hastening to their duties were detained. But when Stilicho discovered the character of his servant he did not wish to punish him, and the men who had been deceived he dismissed at the intervention of the bishop. But to the latter he made complaint of this servant. And the holy man caused him to be sought as he was going out of the Ambrosian Basilica and brought to him. And when he questioned him and discovered him as the author of so great a crime, he said: "He should be given over to Satan for the destruction of his body lest someone in the future should dare commit such deeds." And at the same moment, when the words were still in the mouth of the bishop, the unclean spirit seized him and began to tear him asunder. And at the sight of this we were filled with no small fear and wonder. In these days also, by the imposition of his hands and by his bidding, we saw many cleansed of unclean spirits.

44. At the same time when a certain Nicentius[16] an ex-tribune and notary, so crippled by pain in his feet that he was rarely seen in public, approached the altar to receive the sacraments, and on being stepped upon accidentally by the bishop cried out, he heard the following words: "Go, and henceforth you will be well." That he was no longer troubled with his feet, he testified with tears at the time when the holy bishop departed from this life.

NOTES

1. Evidently according to this passage Ambrose did not always avail himself of a *notarius*, as was the custom among the other writers of this period.

Chapter IX

The custom of having a *notarius* is very old, as we read of Cicero having Tiro, his freedman and his friend, as his stenographer or *notarius*. The *notarii* in the second century were a separate class of officials whose duty it was to take down in shorthand from dictation or public speeches. The *exceptores* were also stenographers but they were employed in the service of the magistrates alone, while the so-called *amanuenses* simply transcribed shorthand records into longhand. From the works of the Fathers we learn that it was a regular custom to have the *notarii* present in the church to take down the sermons as they were being delivered. Cf. Deferrari, Roy J., "Saint Augustine's Method of Composing and Delivering Sermons," *American Journal of Philology*, Volume 42, No. 2, 1922, 97–123.
2. 2 Corinthians 8:9.
3. Romans 12:15.
4. We read that in early ages of Christianity it was a custom with the Christians to practice public confession of their sins. Since sins were confessed publicly, it is evident that there was no need of the seal of confession on the part of the clergy. When then do we first hear of the seal of confession? In the Eastern Church we find Saint Basil (†379) in his Second Canonical Letter to Amphilochius [see Basil the Great, *Letters, Volume 2*, translated by Agnes C. Way] and Saint John Chrysostom in *Homily on Genesis* 20, 3 and in *Homily on the Incomprehensible Nature of God,* 5, 7, writing and speaking emphatically in favor of the seal of confession, considering it a professional obligation.

The Fathers of the Western Church, such as Saint Ambrose and Saint Augustine, were also advocates of the seal of confession. We read (VII according to Mansi, 1, and c. 5 Mansi 4, 4, 38 B) that at the Council of Carthage, held in 419, at which Saint Augustine was present, the first penalty was imposed upon a bishop—for they alone heard confessions then—who violated the seal of confession. But it was not until 459 that the first decretal was issued, enjoining secret confession and absolute silence on the part of the confessor, by Pope Leo the Great. Finally in 1213 at the Council of Lateran under Innocent III (Hefele-Leclerq, *Histoire de Conciles*, II, 2, 1077, and Mansi II, 1007 E), the first official decision, touching the entire Church was issued, expressly prohibiting the confessor to betray the penitent. Honoré, L., *Le Secret de la Confession*, Paris 1924. *Note to the 2019 edition:* The custom of confession in the Roman Church of the 5th century AD is described in some detail by Hermias Sozomen in his Ecclesiastical History, Book VII, Chapter 16.
5. 2 Corinthians 2:8.

6. Proverbs 8:17.
7. 2 Kings 12:13.
8. Psalms 101:10.
9. Psalms 140:4.
10. Deuteronomy 18:2.
11. Luke 16:9.
12. Psalm 136:9. According to the Fathers of the Church this verse is to be interpreted in moral sense. The "little ones" are to be understood as being the first beginnings of faults which being easily conquered, ought to be destroyed at once or while they are yet in an early stage. Cf. Cornelius Lapide, *Commentarii in Sacram Scripturam,* Tom. XIV, 699–700; H. Lesêtre, *La Sainte Bible Le Livre des Psaumes,* 642–643.
13. Psalm 118:57.
14. Matthew 19:29.
15. We read in Tillemont and Baunard that about the year 375 Saint Ambrose founded a *Presbyterium* for the training of the clerics of his diocese. Castus may not have been in charge of the entire *Presbyterium,* but he must have held a distinctive supervisory duty in this model school of Ambrose, since Paulinus gives us to understand that Castus was his superior when he writes "under whose care I lived." According to Paulinus (see below, Chapter 10, section 46), Castus remained a deacon all his life, which often happened in the early ages of Christianity. Cf. Tillemont 263, 279, Baronius, year AD 397, 37–38.
16. An ex-tribune and notary, Nicentius is mentioned also by Saint Ambrose in Letter V, 8, to Syagrius, Bishop of Verona, on a charge falsely brought against the virgin Indicia. Cf. Smith and Wace, *Dictionary of Christian Biography,* IV, 35.

CHAPTER X

HE IS SEIZED WITH SICKNESS AND, REFRESHED WITH THE HOLY VIATICUM, DIES. THE FUNERAL RITES ARE CELEBRATED BY A GREAT GATHERING OF ALL. DEMONS ARE WITNESS TO HIS HOLINESS. HE APPEARS TO MANY AFTER DEATH.

45. But after these days, when a bishop was ordained for the church of Ticinum, he fell ill and while he was being confined to his bed for many days by this illness, Count

Chapter X

Stilicho is reported to have said that with the departure of so great a man from this life, ruin would threaten Italy. Therefore after calling together into his presence the nobles of the city whom he knew were beloved by the bishop, partly with threats and partly with soft words, he persuaded them to go to the holy bishop and induce him to seek of the Lord the privilege of a longer period of life for himself. When he heard this from them he answered: "I have not so lived among you that I am ashamed to live nor do I fear to die, because we have a good Lord!"

46. At the same time when Castus, Polemius,[1] Venerius,[2] and Felix,[3] then deacons, were together in the farthest part of the portico in which he lay, and were conversing among themselves in such a low tone that they could scarcely hear each other, as to who should be consecrated bishop after his death, and when they spoke of the name of Saint Simplicianus,[4] Ambrose as if taking part in the conversation—although he lay placed far away from them—exclaimed thrice in approbation: "Old but good." For Simplicianus was ripe in years. When they heard this voice, they fled greatly terrified. But when he died, no other succeeded him in the episcopacy than he whom he had designated three times as *good but old*. And to this Simplicianus, Venerius was the successor, whom we have mentioned above, while Felix to this day ruled the Church of Bonona. And Castus and Polemius, however, nourished by Ambrose, the good fruits of a good tree, are performing the duties of the diaconate in the church of Milan.

47. In the same place, however, in which he lay, as we have learned from the report of Saint Bassianus[5] the Bishop of the Church of Lodi[6] who had heard it from the Saint himself, when he saw the Lord Jesus advance to him and smiling upon him. And not many days after he was taken from us. But at the very time when he departed from us to

the Lord, from about the eleventh hour of the day until the hour in which he breathed forth his spirit, he prayed with his arms extended in the form of a cross. We indeed saw his lips move but his voice we did not hear. Honoratus[7] also, the bishop of the Church of Vercelli,[8] when he had lain down to rest in the upper part of the house, heard a voice calling him three times and saying to him: "Arise, hasten, because now he is about to depart." And he going down offered the Saint the Body of the Lord and when he took and swallowed it he breathed forth his spirit, bearing with him a good viaticum so that his soul refreshed by virtue of this food now rejoices in the company of the angles, according to whose life he had lived on earth, and in the society of Elias, because just as Elias never feared to speak to kings or any powers, so neither did he for fear of God.

48. And then at the hour before daybreak in which he died, his body was carried to the greater church and it was there on the same night in which we kept the vigil of Easter. And many baptized infants as they were coming from the font saw him, so that some said he was sitting on the throne[9] in the sanctuary,[10] while others pointed him out with their fingers to their parents as walking, but the latter, on looking, were unable to see him because they did not possess clean eyes. And many related, moreover, that they had seen a star over his body. But on Sunday at daybreak when, after the sacred rites had been performed, his body was being taken away from the church to be carried to the Ambrosian Basilica in which it was placed, thereupon a crowd of demons so cried out that they were being tormented by him that their wailing could not be endured. And this grace of the bishop remains even to the present day not only in that place, but also in great many provinces. Crowds of men and women also threw their handkerchiefs or girdles that the body of the Saint might in some way be touched by

Chapter X

them. For the crowd at the obsequies was numberless, of every rank and of every sex and almost all ages, not only of Christians but also of Jews and pagans. Yet the ranks of those who had been baptized led the way because of their greater favor.

49. But on the very day on which he died (as the text of the letter says which was received by his successor, the venerable man Simplicianus, sent from the East to Ambrose himself as if still living with us, which letter even to this day is preserved in a monastery at Milan), he appeared to certain holy men, praying with them and placing his hands upon them. For the letter which was sent has the date, and when we read this letter we found that it was the day on which he died.

50. In Tuscia also in the district of Florence, where now the holy man Zenobius is bishop,[11] we have learned on the report of the holy bishop Zenobius himself that Ambrose, because he had promised those who besought him that he would visit them often, was frequently seen praying at the altar, that is in the Ambrosian basilica which was built there by himself. In the same house also in which he abode when avoiding Eugenius, at the time when Radagaisus[12] was besieging the above mentioned city when already the men of this city utterly despaired of themselves, he appeared in a vision to a certain man and promised that deliverance would come to them on the next day. When the man reported this, the courage of the citizens was raised, for on the next day, on the arrival of Stilicho, then Count, with an army, a victory over the enemy was gained. These things we know on the authority of Pansophia, a religious woman, the mother of the boy Pansophius.[13]

51. To Mascezel[14] also, when in despair of his own safety and that of his army which he was leading against Gildo,[15] Ambrose appeared in a vision at night holding a

staff in his hand. And when Mascezel threw himself at the feet of the holy man, striking the earth with the staff by which he was wont to rule, the old man—for in this guise he had appeared to him—said three times: "Here, here, here," marking a place and gave intelligence to the man, whom he had thought worthy of his visitation so that he should know, that in the very spot in which he has seen the holy bishop of the Lord, he would obtain victory on the third day, and so he confidently began the war and brought it to a close. We, however, while at Milan, learned this on the report of Mascezel himself. For in this province also in which we now live and write, he recounted this very thing to many bishops on whose authority also we thought it safer to add to this book what had been learned by ourself.

52. Also, when at Milan we were receiving with the highest devotion the remains of the martyrs Sisinius and Alexander,[16] who within our own time, that is after the death of Saint Ambrose, obtained the crown of martyrdom during the pagan persecutions in the regions of Anauni,[17] we learned, on the report of a certain blind man who on the same day by touching the casket in which the remains of the saints were carried receiving sight, that in a vision at night he had seen a ship approaching a shore in which there was a multitude of men clothed in white, and that when as they were disembarking on the shore he begged one of the crowd to know who these men were, he learned that they were Ambrose and his companions. And when at the sound of his name he prayed that he might receive light, he heard from him: "Go to Milan and meet my brothers who are about to go there, (naming the day), and you will receive light." For the man was, as he himself asserted, from the shore of Dalmatia, and that he had not come previously to the city before he met the relics of the saints on the main highway, not yet being able to see. But when he touched the bier, he began to see.

Chapter X

NOTES

1. Paulinus seems to be our only source of information on Polemius. Cf. Tillemont, *Historia Ecclesiastica*, Volume X, 263–264 and 279.
2. Saint Venerius succeeded Saint Simplicianus in the see of Milan in 400. He was one of the most distinguished prelates of the time, a friend and supporter of Saint John Chrysostom. Among the letters of the latter, Letter 182 was written to Saint Venerius about 406. His good work for the Church is also mentioned by Pope Saint Anastasius I in Letter II *ad Ioan. Ieresol. Frag. ad Venerium Mediol.* Ennodius (Lit. II, Carm. 79) likewise praised the life and deeds of Saint Venerius. He died in 409 in the ninth year of his episcopate. We celebrate his feast on May 4. Cf. Smith and Wace, *Dictionary of Christian Biography*, IV, 1105 Venerius (1). *Note to the 2019 edition:* For more on Saint Venerius and his possible authorship of the treatise entitled *De Sacramentis*, see Hitchcock, Venerius, Bishop of Milan—II in *Hermathena*, No. 71, May 1948, 19–35.
3. Felix, seventh bishop of Bologna, a native of Milan, was a pupil and deacon of Saint Ambrose. After the war of Theodosius with Eugenius, Saint Ambrose chose Saint Felix as the bearer of a letter to the emperor Theodosius in which he requests the latter to pardon the guilty and the followers of Eugenius. In this letter (Letter 62) Saint Ambrose calls Felix, "my son, the deacon Felix." He became bishop of Bologna about AD 400 and held the see until his death in 429 when he was succeeded by Saint Petronius. Cf. Smith and Wace, *Dictionary of Christian Biography*, II, 488.
4. Saint Simplicianus, the successor of Saint Ambrose in the see of Milan held the see only three years as he was very old when he became bishop. He was highly esteemed by both Saint Ambrose and Saint Augustine and the latter in Letter XXXVII, addresses him as his "father, most worthy of being cherished with respect and sincere affection." Saint Augustine even asks him for criticism of his works which might come into his hands. In Saint Augustine's *City of God* Book X, Chapter 29 and *Confessions* Book VIII, Chapters 1 and 3, we see this great doctor humbly submitting to the fatherly guidance of Saint Simplicianus. To him Saint Augustine wrote two books, *On Various Questions* of which the second bears the special title of *To Simplician.*

Among the Letters of Saint Ambrose there are four addressed to Saint Simplicianus: Letters XXXVII, XXXVIII, LXV, and LXVII. Letter LXV he concludes with *Vale, et nos parentis affectu dilige, ut facis,* (Farewell, and love me as you do with the affection of a parent) which shows us the warm affection of Saint Ambrose for Saint Simplicianus. He died AD 400 and we celebrate his feast

August 16. Cf. Tillemont X, 397–406; Smith and Wace, *Dictionary of Christian Biography*, IV, 688–689; *Catholic Encyclopedia*, X, 300.

5. Saint Bassianus, Bishop of Lodi, was one of the bishops who condemned the Arians, Palladius and Secundianus, as heretics, at the Council of Aquileia. Cf. Ambrose, *Gesta Concillii Aquileiensis Contra Palladium et Secundianum Hœreticos*. The proceedings of this council are found in English in *The Letters of Saint Ambrose, Bishop of Milan*, as translated by Walford. He is also mentioned by Saint Ambrose in Letter IV to Felix, bishop of Como, inviting him to the consecration of a church by Bassianus. Saint Bassianus died in AD 413 and was buried in the church which he dedicated in honor of the Holy Apostles at Lodi, of which city he is the patron saint. His feast is celebrated January 19. Cf. Smith and Wace, *Dictionary of Christian Biography*, I, 298.

6. Lodi, the capital of a district in the province of Milan, is situated on the right bank of the Adda. It is reported that under Diocletian, about 4,000 Christians with their bishop, whose name is unknown, were burned in their church. In the Middle Ages, Lodi was second to Milan among the cities of northern Italy. Cf. *Catholic Encyclopedia*, IX, 322; Baedeker's *Northern Italy*, 299.

7. Honoratus, bishop of Vercelli succeeded Limenius bishop, who was the immediate successor of Saint Eusebius. He received his education in the Presbyterium founded by Saint Eusebius and faithfully followed his master and teacher in his zeal for orthodoxy. He was an intimate friend of Saint Paulinus of Nola as well as of Saint Ambrose to whom he administered the Holy Viaticum at his last hour. His feast is celebrated October 29. Cf. Smith and Wace, *Dictionary of Christian Biography*, III, 137–138.

8. The archdiocese of Vercelli is in the province of Novara, Piedmont, Italy. Saints Sabinianus and Martialis, bishops from Gaul, according to ancient legend, were the first to preach the Gospel here in the second half of the third century. The episcopal see, however, was not established until after the peace of Constantine. Saint Eusebius, a Sardinian, a lector of the Roman Church and a strenuous opponent of Arianism, was its first bishop. Cf. *Catholic Encyclopedia*, XV, 384–389.

9. Originally, *cathedra* meant a chair used by rhetors in giving their instructions in school. Later this chair was transferred into the church and was used by the bishop, immediately taking on a liturgical meaning. Wherever a bishop placed his *cathedra*, or chair, that church became the episcopal church or the official seat of the bishop, hence our present-day term, cathedral. From this

Chapter X

point on, the *cathedra* and church became inseparable and created an ecclesiastical unity or diocese. In the second half of the fourth century the *cathedra* was elevated and could be reached only by ascending steps. Cf. Cabrol, *Dictionnaire D'archéologie Chrétienne et de Liturgie,* III, 19–75; also T. L. L. III, 612, 1 ff.

10. The sanctuary is the space in the church containing the main altar. Around the sanctuary there may be "stalls" or seats for the clergy. This part of the church was variously designated *tribuna* or tribunal, being one of the many names given to it. Cf. *Catholic Encyclopedia,* XIII, 431-432; Cabrol, *Dictionnaire D'archéologie Chrétienne et de Liturgie* I, 183–197.

11. Saint Zenobius, Bishop of Florence, was a friend of Saint Ambrose, and much esteemed by Pope Saint Damasus. Being a pagan, he came under the influence of Bishop Theodore, who baptized him. Later he embraced the clerical state and his virtues and power as a teacher brought him to the attention of Saint Ambrose and Pope Damasus. The latter employed him in various important missions. Antoninus, his successor and biographer, tells us that he died in his nineteenth year in 424. His feast is celebrated May 24. Cf. *Catholic Encyclopedia,* XV, 755.

12. Radagaisus, leader of the Germanic tribe, was a Scythian according to Jornandes. He invaded Italy in 406 and after destroying many towns and laying siege to Florence he was hemmed in by Stilicho. Owing to the shortness of provisions he was compelled to come forth and join in battle. He was driven back and capitulated and finally put to death. His followers were sold as slaves. Cf. Smith, *Dictionary of Greek and Roman Biography and Mythology,* III, 640; *Cambridge Mediaeval History, Volume I, The Christian Roman Empire,* 265.

13. *Note to the 2019 edition:* Pansophia is the mother of the boy Pansophius who Saint Ambrose raised from the dead according to the present account by Paulinus. See Chapter 8, paragraph 28.

14. Mascezel, brother of Gildo, was placed by Stilicho at the head of the Roman troops because of his bravery in the revolt of Firmus. He was sent with 36,000 men against Gildo, who in 398, refusing to allow the grain from Africa to be transported to Rome, brought about this Gildonic War. Mascezel was successful in this war, as the whole army of Gildo surrendered themselves up to him. He did not long survive his brother for, as history tells us, Stilicho, envious of this success of Mascezel, threw him off a bridge into a river to drown. Cf. Smith, *Dictionary of Greek and Roman Biography and Mythology,* II, 267–268; *Cambridge Mediaeval History, Volume 1, Christian Roman Empire,* 263.

15. Gildo was a Moor by birth, the son of Nubel and brother of Firmus. This Firmus revolted against the Romans during the reign of Valentinian I. Though Gildo helped put down Firmus's revolt and was rewarded, he himself rebelled during the reign of Honorius. War broke out in 398 when he refused to allow the grain crops to be conveyed to Rome. This war is vividly described by Claudian in his *De Bello Gildonico*. The author calls him a tyrant, detestable for cruelty and avarice. Stilicho fitted out the expedition and placed Mascezel at the head of the army, who had cruel wrongs of his own to avenge upon Gildo, his brother. The latter was defeated by Mascezel and according to Gibbon, C, XXIX, died by his own hand, but other historians seem to believe that he was murdered. Cf. Smith and Wace, *Dictionary of Christian Biography,* II, 672; Smith, *Dictionary of Greek and Roman Biography and Mythology,* II, 267–268; *Cambridge Mediaeval History, Volume I, Christian Roman Empire*, 262–264.

16. Sisinius, Alexander, and Martyricus were martyred by the pagans at Anaunia, near Trent. Sisinnius, a Greek from Cappadocia, ordained deacon by Vigilius, bishop of Trent, was then sent to convert the neighboring pagans to Christianity, as they still worshipped Saturn. The account of the sufferings of these martyrs is found in two extant letters written by Vigilius, one to Saint Simplicianus of Milan and the other to Saint John Chrysostom. We celebrate their feast May 29. Cf. Smith and Wace, *Dictionary of Christian Biography,* IV, 704; *Catholic Encyclopedia,* XI, 338; XV, 426.

17. Anauni was a canton about ten leagues from Trent to the northwest, along the river which today is called La Noce. Cf. Tillemont, X, 542. *In Anauniæ partibus*: on *partes—regiones*. Cf. Sec. 22, n. 4.

CHAPTER XI

GOD SAFEGUARDS THE MEMORY OF THE HOLY BISHOP AGAINST DETRACTORS. AN EXHORTATION ON IMITATING HIM. THE AUTHOR'S EPILOGUE.

53. And so having discussed these matters I do not think it will appear offensive if we exceed a little the bounds of our promise, that we may show that the word of the Lord which He spoke through the mouths of the holy prophets has been fulfilled: *The man that sitteth against his brother and*

Chapter XI

detracteth him in private will I persecute.[1] And elsewhere: *Love not to detract, lest you be totally destroyed,*[2] so that whoever by chance is seized by a habit of this kind, when he has read how vengeance has been taken on those who dared to detract from the holy man, himself also among others may be corrected.

54. Now a certain Donatus,[3] an African by race but a presbyter of the church of Milan, when seated at a banquet at which were some religious soldiers, he detracted from the memory of the bishop—although they spurned and avoided his wretched tongue—was suddenly struck with a severe wound. He was raised up by strange hands from the place in which he lay, placed on a litter, and carried thence even to the grave. In the city of Carthage also when I had gone to the house of the deacon Fortunatus, brother of the venerable bishop Aurelius,[4] to dine together with Vincentius,[5] bishop of Colositanum,[6] with Muranus[7] also bishop of Bolita,[8] and other bishops and deacons, to Bishop Muranus who was then detracting from the holy man I related the fate of the presbyter mentioned above. And these words concerning another he confirmed as an oracle about himself by his own premature death. For, after he had been suddenly struck with a great wound, from the very place on which he lay he was carried by strange hands to a bed. And on being brought thence to the house in which he was a guest brought his days to a close. This was the end of men who detract him, and those who were then present on seeing this marveled.

55. Wherefore, I urge and beseech every man who will read this book, to imitate the life of the man, to praise the grace of God, and to avoid the tongues of detractors if he wishes rather to have companionship with Ambrose in the resurrection of life, than with those detractors to undergo a punishment which no wise man does not avoid.

56. I also beg your Blessedness,[9] father Augustine, that

for me, the most humble man and sinner Paulinus, together with all the saints who with you invoke the name of Our Lord Jesus Christ in truth, you may deign to pray, so that since in obtaining grace, I am not worthy to have companionship with so great a man, having obtained pardon for my sins, I may receive the reward of escaping punishment.

NOTES

1. Psalms 100:5.
2. Proverbs 20:13.
3. Donatus was a presbyter of Milan but African by birth. This seems to be his only mention in ancient literature. Cf. Tillemont, X, 267.
4. Saint Aurelius, archbishop of Carthage from 388 to 423, was a fellow worker of Saint Augustine. During his episcopate we hear of the first beginnings of Pelagianism as well as the great struggles of the Donatists to uphold their sect. He met and withstood both these blows with decision and wisdom. He denounced Pelagianism by excommunicating and driving Cœlestius, a disciple of Pelagius, from Carthage. In 416 both Coelestius and Pelagius were condemned in a synod held at Carthage. We find him mentioned in the African martyrology on July 20. Cf. *Catholic Encyclopedia,* II, 108.
5. Vincentius was the bishop of Culusitanum and the main factor in the Carthaginian Conference held in 411. In 407 he joined Fortunatus of Sicca in a mission to Honorius to request that representatives be appointed for the support of the causes of the African Church before the imperial tribunal. Again in 418 he was chosen from the province of Carthage as a member of the judicial committee, consisting of three bishops from each province, to act on behalf of the African episcopate. He was also present at a council held at Carthage in 419. Cf. Smith and Wace, *Dictionary of Christian Biography,* IV, 1154.
6. Culcitanum, Cullicitanum or Culusitanum is a place in the pro-consular province of Africa, but placed between Rusiccada and Hippo by Antoninus. We learn of bishops being named from that place for the years 348 (Mansi, Act. Con. III, 147), 411 (Mansi, IV, 123), 419 (Mansi 419, 433, 436, 508, 509). In some places it is mentioned as Culsitanum rather than Culusitanum. The references from the year 484 and 649 show that is was a town belonging to a pro-consular province. Cf. Mansi, VIII, 647, 649, Vol. X, 940. Also P.-Wissowa, Vol. IV, 1754.
7. Muranus, bishop of Bolita is likely mentioned only in this passage.
8. Bolita, in ancient times known as Volita, is in the province of

Chapter XI

Zeugitana, otherwise called Proconsular Africa. Cf. Bingham, J., *Antiques of the Christian Church,* I, 412-413; also Pauly-Wissowa III, 675.

9. Blessedness (or *beatitudinem* in Latin) is a title of honor especially in speaking of or addressing a bishop.

INDEX

Æmilia 5, 8
Agricola, saint 32, 39–40
Alexander, martyr 52, 56
Altar of Victory 23, 30, 37–38
Ambrose, father of Saint Ambrose 3
Ambrosian Basilica 3, 6, 17, 46, 50–51
Anaunia 52, 56
Anemius 11, 13–14
Anthony the Abbot, saint xviii, xxvii, 1
Aquileia xvii, 13, 23–24, 27, 33, 54
Arbogast iv, 23, 30, 32–33, 38–39
Arcadius, emperor 41
Arians i, 8, 10, 13, 15–18, 27, 54
Athanasius, saint xviii, xxii, 1, 12
Augustine, saint iii–iv, xii–xiv, xviii–xix, xxi, xxvi, 1, 6, 16, 19–20, 37, 47, 53, 58, 71
Aurelius, bishop xiv, xv, 57–58
Auxentius, Arian bishop of Milan 8, 11–13

Basilica of the Apostles 34
Bassianus, saint iv, xxviii, 49, 54
Bolita 57, 59
Bologna (*also Bononia*) xii, xix, xxviii, 30, 32, 39, 40, 53

Candida 4, 5, 6
Carthage xiii–xv 4, 6, 24, 47, 57–58, 71
Castus xii, 45, 48–49
Celsus, saint xiii, 34, 40–41
Cœlestius, heretic xiv–xvi, xxi
Colositanum 57
Cresconius 35, 41

Dalmatia 52
Damascus 9

Decens 31
Dionysius, saint, Bishop of Milan 8, 11–12
Donatus 57–58

Eugenius, emperor iv, 30, 32–33, 38–40, 51, 53
Eusebius, prefect 35, 41
Eusebius, saint 54
Euthymius 14

Faventia (*also Faenza*) 30, 39
Felix, bishop of Bologna xii, xix, xxviii, 49, 53–54,
Felix, martyr 16, 19
Flavian 30, 33, 38
Fortunatus xiv, 57–58
Franks 32
Frigitil, queen of the Macromanni 36

Gervase, saint i, 3, 16, 19
Gildo 51, 55–56
Gratian, emperor iv, 7, 13–14, 18, 23, 36–38, 42

Honorius, emperor 35, 40–41, 56, 58

Innocent, sooth-sayer 21, 24
Innocent I, Pope xv, xix, xxi, 47
Isidore of Seville, saint xii, xvi, 6
Italy 5, 7–8, 13, 20, 23, 28, 30, 36, 38–39, 41, 44, 49, 54–55

Jerome, saint xviii, xxii, xxvii, 1
Jews 9, 17–18, 24, 28, 32, 51
John, prefect xix, xxvii, 33, 40,
John Chrysostom, saint 47, 53, 56
Justina, empress i, iv, 3, 11, 14, 17, 21–23

The Life of Saint Ambrose

Leontius 10
Libya 35
Liguria 5, 7–8
Lodi xxviii, 13, 54

Macedonius 36, 42
Marcellina, saint xxviii, 1, 3, 6, 15, 19, 20, 29,
Marcomanni 30, 36, 41
Marius Mercator xii, xxvi
Martin, saint xviii, xx, xxv, xxvii, 1, 3
Mascezel 51, 52, 55, 56
Maximus, Magnus, emperor i, 21, 23–24, 42
Milan xii, xvi, xix, xxvi, xxvii, 1, 3, 5, 8–16, 19–20, 22–26, 30, 32–33, 35–37, 39–40, 49, 51–54, 56–58
miracles xx, xxii, 4, 8, 19–20
Muranus, bishop xiv, 57, 59,
Mutina (*also Modena*) 36, 41

Nabor, saint 16, 19
Nazarius, saint xiii, 33, 40–41
Nicentius 46, 48

Pansophia 51, 55
Pansophius 31, 51, 55
Paulinus, deacon. Author of the *Vita* xi–xxviii, 1–3, 20, 29, 41, 48, 53, 54–55, 58
Paul the Hermit, saint xviii, xxvii, 1
Pelagian heresy xi–xii, xiv–xv
Pelagius, heretic xiv–xv, 58
Persians i, 24, 26
Polemius xii, 49, 53
Portian Basilica 15, 18
Probus 5, 7, 9, 22, 27
Protase, saint i, 3, 16, 19

Radagaisus 51, 55
Rufinus, ecclesiastical historian 29
Rufinus of Aquileia xvi

Serverus, a blind man 17
Sicily xv
Simplicianus, saint xix, xxviii, 49, 51, 53–54, 56
Sirmium 11, 13–14
Sisinius, martyr 52, 56
Stilicho 35, 41, 46, 49, 51, 55–56
Suebi 41
Suetonius xxiv
Sulpicius Severus xviii, xx, xxv, xxvii, 3, 42,
Symmachus i, 30, 36–38, 42

Theodosius I, emperor i, 3, 23–24, 28–30, 32–33, 37–41, 53
Theodulus, notary and bishop 36, 41
Thessalonica i, xxi, 24, 26
Tiber River 10
Ticinum 9, 12–13, 48
Tuscia 30, 32, 39, 51

Valens, emperor 13–14, 23, 41
Valentinians, heretical sect 24, 27, 28
Valentinian I, emperor 6–7, 9, 12–14, 22–23, 37, 56
Valentinian II, emperor 3, 7, 14, 21, 23, 30, 37–39
Venerius, saint xii, xix, xxviii, 49, 53
Vercelli xxviii, 50, 54,
Vienna 30
Vincentius 57–58
Vitalis, father of Saints Gervase and Protase 19
Vitalis, saint 32, 39–40

Zenobius, saint xix, xxviii, 51, 55
Zosimus, Pope xv, xvi, xxi, xxvi

Also available in the *Christian Roman Empire* Series

Volume 1. *The Life of Belisarius,* by Lord Mahon

Volume 2. *The Gothic History of Jordanes: In English Version with an Introduction and a Commentary,* Translated by Charles Mierow

Volume 3. *The Book of the Popes (Liber Pontificalis): To the Pontificate of Gregory I,* Translated by Louise Ropes Loomis

Volume 4. *The Chronicle of John, Bishop of Nikiu: Translated from Zotenberg's Ethiopic Text,* Translated by R. H. Charles

Volume 5. *The Ecclesiastical Annals of Evagrius: A History of the Church from AD 431 to AD 594,* Translated by Edward Walford

Volume 6. *The Life of Saint Augustine: A Translation of the* Sancti Augustini Vita *by Possidius, Bishop of Calama,* Translated by Herbert T. Weiskotten

Volume 7. *The Life of Saint Simeon Stylites: A Translation of the Syriac in* Bedjan's Acta Martyrum et Sanctorum, Translated by Rev. Frederick Lent

Volume 8. *The Life of the Blessed Emperor Constantine: In Four Books from 306 to 337 AD,* by Eusebius Pamphilus

Volume 9. *The Dialogues of Saint Gregory the Great* edited by Edmund G. Gardner

Volume 10. *The Complete Works of Saint Cyprian of Carthage,* edited by Phillip Campbell

Volume 11. *The Fragmentary History of Priscus: Attila, the Huns and the Roman Empire, AD 430-476,* translated with an introduction by John Given

Volume 12. *The Ecclesiastical History of Sozomen: From AD 324 to AD 425,* Translated by Edward Walford

For more information on this series, see our website at:
http://www.evolpub.com/CRE/CREseries.html

www.ingramcontent.com/pod-product-compliance
Lightning Source LLC
Chambersburg PA
CBHW021021090426
42738CB00007B/854